# a Day in May

*To the 1,201,607 people who voted 'Yes'*
*in the Marriage Equality referendum*
*in Ireland on 22 May 2015.*

## Real Lives, True Stories

## Charlie Bird

### Edited by Kevin Rafter

*With a Foreword by Colm Tóibín*

MERRION
PRESS

Published in 2016 by
Merrion Press
8 Chapel Lane
Sallins
Co. Kildare

British Library Cataloguing in Publication Data
An entry can be found on request

978-1-78537-076-2 (Cloth)
978-1-78537-077-9 (PDF)
978-1-78537-079-3 (Kindle)

Library of Congress Cataloging in Publication Data
An entry can be found on request

Designed by Clío Meldon at Language.

Endpapers: © Peter Morrison/AP/Press Association Images

Extract on page one taken from "Replenishing Fountain", *Station
Island* (1984) © Estate of Seamus Heaney and reprinted by permission
of Faber and Faber Ltd. and Farrar, Straus and Giroux, LLC.

# Contents

# *Foreword*

## *Colm Tóibín*

Most communities who have been oppressed have had every opportunity to work out the implications of the oppression in their early lives. As children, they hear the stories; they have the books around them or the ballads. Gay people, on the other hand, grow up alone. There are no ballads about the wrongs of our past; the martyrs are all forgotten. It is as though, in the words of the gay American poet Adrienne Rich's phrase 'you looked into the mirror and saw nothing'. Thus the discovery of a gay history and of a gay tradition and a sense of gay heritage has to be done by each individual as part of the road to freedom.

Gay history is a set of lonely shadows, dotted lines, stories not told, isolated suffering, silences and marginalisations. Thus the idea of individual witness and the idea of each gay person having a story to tell go beyond the personal into the political. It moves our lives from shadow into substance. It creates a sense of community and joins the dotted lines of history. It offers us not only an image of others, but of ourselves.

As with all stories of slow, gradual liberation, there have been some unlikely enabling spirits and some odd and ambiguous heroes on the road towards acceptance of gay people in Ireland. In the early 1980s, it would have seemed absurd to claim that gay people in Ireland would move into the light courtesy of the Irish Constitution of 1937, since it was that very document that allowed the Supreme Court, in a three-two judgment, to dismiss the case which David Norris brought as an Irish citizen and a gay man who sought to have his rights vindicated.

Yet these stories collected by Charlie Bird, filled with bracing honesty and heart-breaking personal revelation, make clear that being gay in Ireland was perhaps a more essential aspect of Irish history and Irish reality than anyone was aware. These stories tell of an anguish that arises from silence and intolerance and fear. This was a feeling experienced also by many women in Ireland, and indeed by children. It was a feeling shared by those who belonged to the travelling community, by immigrants and by other who were treated as an underclass or outcasts.

On reading these gay histories and testimonies, in all their clarity and intensity, it is obvious that only a national referendum on the right of gay people to be equal in Ireland could have come close to repairing the damage that was done and setting a new agenda in Ireland. We needed a discussion that would make its way into every town and county in the country, every home and every individual conscience. An act of parliament might have been helpful, but it would not have had the same overwhelming effect as a referendum campaign that would depend on individual witness and personal stories.

The central idea behind the 'Yes' campaign was to show civility rather than anger, to use a soft tone. The campaign wished to make clear that we, as gay people, wanted to belong, that we are Irish as well as gay, and members of families who love us before we are anything. We had suffered enough, in any case, from incivility.

In a way, we took the word love from those who had belittled our love, and we reclaimed it. This meant that the people who spoke in the campaign did not propose anything abstract or philosophical, but instead adopted a tone that was honest, personal, true. The campaign just asked its canvassers to tell particular, concrete stories, or let others do so. The aim was to make things personal rather than political, to make the campaign local rather than national, to ask for votes one at a time.

Gay people in Ireland wanted to offer the electorate both excitement and stability. We wanted to ask some people to have the imagination to change their minds, which is itself an exciting process, but we also wanted to emphasise that we wished to enhance what was already there in the best aspects of Ireland – tolerance, easy-going attitudes, caring for your neighbour. While the campaign was modern and slick, it was also old-fashioned and traditional as people went from door to door or used local forums to make their arguments. Central to its success was the working with parents and grandparents, the allowing of gay people to be seen with their loving families.

In the euphoria of winning the referendum campaign, it is important to remember the amount of suffering which rejection and marginalisation caused to gay people in Ireland. And it is important to bear in mind also, in listening to the voices assembled here, that there has been a great deal of prejudice, that many people among us have been willing to be cruel. Discrimination seemed to be almost everyday, almost casual, part of the fabric of the society. It will take more than a single campaign or a single referendum to change things fully in Ireland.

The importance of this book is to show how rich and interesting and utterly individual each gay voice is, and how unique and different each experience of being gay in Ireland has been. Yet there are certain things that stand out and seem to have been part of a pattern. Mainly fear and silence. But also bullying and a deep sense of aloneness. Both the referendum and this collection of voices themselves will help and empower anyone who is starting out their lives as gay citizens in Ireland, but the tone of some of these voices here, and the texture, will make clear that maybe what we have now is only a beginning, a road-map to freedom. There is much work still to be done to make Ireland a more relaxed and equal place for its gay citizens.

*Colm Tóibín is the author of eight novels including* Blackwater Lightship, The Master *and* The Testament of Mary, *all three of which were nominated for the Booker Prize. His most recent novels include* Brooklyn *and* Nora Webster.

# Beginnings

*Charlie Bird*

*'The dazzle of the impossible suddenly*
*blazed across the threshold'*

– Seamus Heaney

Dublin Castle. 23 May 2015. A day in May. One glorious day. Hours earlier I had seen the votes tumble out of ballot boxes in the RDS in Dublin. Around Ireland others were witnessing the same history being made. The referendum on marriage equality was going to deliver a 'Yes' majority. In Dublin Castle as the national result was announced joyous scenes met this decisive decision. The world saw Ireland in a whole new light.

It is fair to say I was one of the many caught up in this moment. For almost four decades I had worked as a journalist with RTÉ, the Irish national broadcaster. In that time I had never been involved in any campaigns in what might loosely be called the political arena. I retired from RTÉ in 2013, and having left the station I was free of any constraints on campaigning on particular issues or promoting specific causes. But as I got involved in a number of post-RTÉ projects I didn't rush to be associated with any particular organisation or cause.

Then an invitation came my way. Bride Rosney, a long-time friend and former RTÉ colleague, asked if I would chair a meeting for a group being formed to campaign for a 'Yes' vote in the marriage equality referendum. That is where my association with the referendum started, where my own journey began and where the idea for his book was ultimately born.

My decision to chair the meeting was met by an odd reaction from someone I knew well. Commenting to another friend, this person remarked, 'Will people not think that Charlie is gay?' Even on the cusp of this historic vote some perceptions were still one-dimensional.

All sorts of people, from all sorts of backgrounds, gathered on 9 March 2015 to launch the National Yes Equality campaign for Civil Marriage. We met in the Pillar Room of the Rotunda Hospital in Dublin. This building has over the past 250 years been connected with many momentous events. Situated just off the top of O'Connell Street, in November 1913 it played host to the formation of the Irish Volunteers, who played such a key role in the 1916 Rising, which eventually saw Ireland gaining its independence.

In the spring of 2015, another type of freedom was under discussion in the Pillar Room. Those supporting the campaign were seeking to write another piece of history by making Ireland the first country in the world to vote by popular mandate for marriage equality.

The organisers of the event had arranged that the first part of the meeting would feature four people telling their own stories: Patrick Dempsey, a gay man; Lora Bolger and Gillian McKenna, a lesbian couple; and Enda Morgan, the father of a young gay woman.

My job was to interview each of these people. I had never met any of them previously. We chatted briefly before the meeting got underway. I explained that we would have a short conversation about the importance of the referendum for each of them.

My task was straightforward but I was a little nervous as I went up onto the stage. The Pillar Room was packed. I was asking questions but I was no longer in my familiar role of journalist. I also knew the referendum was deeply personal for many of the people in the room.

I don't think I did a particularly good job of chairing the meeting. But then something amazing happened as Enda Morgan was describing how his daughter Rachel had come out to himself and his wife five years earlier. Enda's story opens this book. His words were so powerful when I heard him speak them, and they inspired me on the journey to this book.

I can still recall the moment. In simplest of terms, without any drama or embellishment, Enda Morgan told us how his daughter was shaking and crying uncontrollably as she told her parents that she was gay. There wasn't a sound in the Pillar Room. The words were powerful: 'to hold your daughter in her twenties in your arms like that, as a parent is, very very distressing and what distressed me most was Rachel bottled this up for quite a number of years.'

At one point Enda paused and said, 'Charlie I'm sorry I'm going on.' To which I replied, 'I want you to, go on.' In that one moment the whole gathering broke into sustained applause. You could feel a wave of emotion move across the whole room.

It is a moment I will never forget. A father's love for his daughter. It encapsulated everything that was important about the marriage equality referendum.

I left the campaign launch energised. I wanted to contribute my little bit to achieving a 'Yes' majority. In the following weeks I chaired seven other meetings across the country where people came to tell their stories. These were open forum meetings where those attending could say why they were voting 'Yes' or, indeed, 'No'. In reality only those in favour of the referendum turned up. But each meeting had a remarkable affect on me, and I also think on everyone who attended.

Mothers, fathers, brothers, sisters, young and old – they all spoke with emotion and love for their lesbian and gay children and the effect of 'their coming out'. Those who were gay and lesbian spoke about the importance of the referendum and what passing the referendum would mean to them personally.

At the meeting in the National Library of Ireland in central Dublin, Anne Rigney from Co. Roscommon read a poem. She had written the words for her son who is gay.

### *Imagine it's your child*

*Imagine you are out for a night with friends and you hear in the background someone at the bar calling a man at the bar, 'Queer', 'Fag' and worse.*

*And Imagine your son is gay.*

*Imagine it is your child and how would you feel. Imagine people smirking at the idea of your son getting married to the person he loves.*

*Imagine it's your child and how would you feel.*

In a small crowded café in Ballinasloe in Co. Galway towards the end of the evening a man indicated to me that he wanted to speak. An elderly man, he first apologised for not standing up due to some medical issues. He had lived all his life in Co. Galway. He had a revelation for everyone in the room. At the age of seventy-two he had finally come out. He recalled how a year or so earlier he had attended a dinner dance organised by the LGBT society in NUI Galway. He said it had been, 'one of the happiest' nights of his life.

There were other remarkable stories at these meetings. These stories inspired the idea for *A Day in May*. When the referendum was won, and the wonderful emotional count day was over, I decided to go back around the country recording the stories of people I'd met during the campaign. The stories are the inspiration for this book and the companion play of the same name.

I recorded almost eighty interviews, over half of which are included in this book. All of these people agreed to be involved. Kevin Rafter edited the interview transcripts and wrote the material into the stand-alone stories published in this book. All the content is drawn from the first-hand accounts of the interviewees. It is never easy to tell a complete stranger the story of your life. It is even harder to talk about things you've never spoken about before. Not all of the stories have come from members of the LGBT community and their families. Some have come from people who played a part in the campaign itself.

Jennifer Tedstone was one of those involved in the referendum campaign. I met her in Buncrana in Co. Donegal. She teaches in a local primary school. She told me about a young gay man in the town who tragically took his own life. 'I knew that he had suffered some abuse from people and the public, but I didn't realise the extent until after he passed away,' Jennifer said. She was motivated to get involved in the campaign after hearing a radio report on Newstalk speculating that Donegal would vote 'No'. Jennifer was disheartened about that possibility. And so, this woman who had never been involved in any political activity decided she needed 'to do something.'

Using Facebook Jennifer organised a highly successful gathering for Yes Equality in Buncrana. Hundreds from all over Donegal turned up. 'It was brilliant, it was such a good day, and people were very emotional,' she recalled. One of the people Jennifer contacted was the playwright Frank McGuinness who comes originally from Buncrana.

He wasn't able to attend the event but did write a powerful speech, which was read out on the day.

> *I wish I could be there to stand and hold your hands on the shorefront of Buncrana. I thank you for taking the time to show this gesture of support. I hope your presence here tells every young gay man, lesbian, bisexual and transgender person you are not alone. We are as many as those who love us. You can stand up and say, I am everyone's equal, I reject lies, I will not be bullied, I am part of a family, a genuine family, that is proud of me for what I am, and not one that diminishes me. Cruelty takes many forms, and violence against LGBT people goes deep. We need to say out loud this cruelty must stop. The violence, verbal, physical, spiritual, must cease. We look you in the face and say we are your own. Can you do the same for us? Harm us, you harm yourself. You harm your children. Wolfe Tone once landed on this very shore to play his part in the great fight for our freedom, for the equality of all. Now, the common name of Irishman and Irishwoman, I ask you to vote yes.*

Another person who I met when travelling around the country in 2015 was Beibhinn O'Connor who helped organise the 'Yes' campaign in Co. Galway. I wrongly assumed Beibhinn was lesbian. Of course, I was jumping to the wrong conclusion. The lesson I learned was that not everyone involved in the campaign came from the LGBT community. Indeed what was most empowering about the 'Yes' campaign was the fact that it drew people from every corner of Irish civil society. Beibhinn was a good example. With one of her friends, Sarah Clancy, Beibhinn was worried that during the early stages of the campaign the main political parties were not doing enough for a 'Yes' vote.

> *I didn't want to wake up the day after the referendum to a 'No' vote and realise that I'd sat on my backside and did nothing about it. And I didn't want to live in that Ireland, you know, that would vote 'No' to this. It was just a straightforward thing, as far as I am concerned.*

While Beibhinn has many LGBT friends she told me it wasn't just for them that she got involved in the campaign. She saw passing the referendum as part of a modern Ireland. Beibhinn explained about some of the abuse canvassers had received on the doorsteps:

> *After our first time out on the doorsteps we realised that actually some of the reactions were appalling. And again I am not gay, so when people were throwing holy water at me, they weren't personally insulting me. But most of the people who were on the canvas were gay. And so it was very much attacking them and who they are and we knew straight away that we had to set up a counselling service.*

There were also lighthearted stories. One person told me about a friend knocking on a door in a small community in rural Ireland. This man whose daughter is lesbian was canvassing in his own locality. He was on the doorstep of a local woman when she asked him why he was canvassing for a 'Yes' vote. When she heard that his daughter was gay this neighbour replied, 'Oh my God, and when was she diagnosed.' Not all the stories I heard were so benign. One young man told me that when he told his parents he was gay his father rang him a few days later asking him to take a DNA test to prove he was his child.

While the Catholic Church made known its opposition to marriage equality, some priests did speak out in favour of a 'Yes' vote. Some of these individuals were well known. Others were low-profile curates in local parishes. In some instances, they came under pressure from their bishop and from some of their parishioners.

I met a local priest who had told his congregation that he was going to support the referendum: 'I was always conscious of the referendum and just listening to different debates and different opinions and so forth, I just felt in my heart that it was the right thing for me to vote yes.'

These views didn't go down to well with his bishop and a minority of the local people. He received letters asking how he could go completely against nature and against God's law. One woman phoned him and asked, 'How can you be a priest?' She said there was a 'darkness' working in his life. Another person said he should be ashamed and 'should take off your collar and look for a day job'. This priest told me that he prayed about his decision to vote 'Yes'.

> *I remember at times sitting in the church on my own in the evenings and at night, just before locking up the church in darkness and I would have been moved by the spirit. There is a line in the mass where the Lord says take this...all of you...and drink from it. And I remember thinking at the time, about this, that this is Christ...take this all of you. It's not saying this is just for some of you, for those who are straight or those who are gay or those who are lesbian or whatever.*

The priest recalled the day of the referendum result and his response to the outcome:

> *I cried that day. I shed a tear. I was saying, 'Thank you, God.' It was just the joy of it. And just to look at the news that night to see the people. My little vote of 'Yes' added to their joy, their celebration. And I said, 'Thank you, God. It was very much worth it.'*

Before that day in May 2015 there were darker times. David Norris' successful European Court case and the subsequent decriminalisation of homosexuality in 1993 were landmark moments. But these advances also came at a cost. Brian Sheehan, the Executive Director of GLEN – the Gay and Lesbian Equality Network – recalls an earlier era with zero visibility. 'The only time you ever saw it in the newspapers was in a pejorative sense. So there was the Declan Flynn murder and there was Charles Self.'

As a young researcher in RTÉ, in 1979 I had worked with Charles Self on a special *Late Late Show* from London. He was the set designer on the show for many years. He was a well-known figure in the gay community and was murdered in his south Dublin apartment in January 1982. At one time Charles had shared the house with another person I had also known, Vincent Hanley. Vincent was affectionally known as 'Fab Vinnie'. He was the well-known presenter of the popular MT-USA television programme. Vincent died from an AIDS-related illness in 1987.

In the *Sunday Independent* in July 2011, the newspaper's security editor, Jim Cusack said that Garda homophobia played a part in the failure to solve the case. 'Old fashioned homophobic bigotry on the part of some Gardaí, not involved in the investigation towards the gay community in the early '80s, may well have played a part in the failure to solve Dublin's most high profile gay killing in 1982.' Brian Sheehan mentioned how the Gardaí got hold of Charles Self's contact book after the murder and had begun to question those whose names appeared in the book. This created a climate of fear.

> *The police turned up at your home, at your place of work to interview you and suddenly and that's a lot of where the profound mistrust of the police came from, is that, a*

*whole community who couldn't be open, because they were illegal suddenly felt that the state, through the arms of the police were out to get them. I have no idea if it's true but I have heard a number of times people say that specific people died by suicide because they were already under intolerable pressure in their own lives and suddenly the police were turning up. And the police did it to intimidate. So the culture was, it was OK, it was a bit like the heavy gang were out raiding houses and you know turning up at people who were suspected of being in the IRA. So it was the same kind of approach to people who were in Charles Self's circle of friends and wider. And it literally terrified people you know.*

Bill Hughes, the television producer, whose story is included in this book, recalls coming out in the late nineteen seventies and what he describes as the 'witch hunt' of members of the gay community in the wake of the murder of Charles Self. Bill recalls that some Gardaí were, 'outing people within their work place. People were resigning from work and jumping on ferries and planes and any way they could get out of this country and where they could live their lives normally.'

Times change and attitudes evolve. The decision of the Irish people in May 2015 makes that case so powerfully. The stories in this book capture intimately how people's life experience has affected them as an LGBT person, both positive and negative.

Many talk about the difficulties they had in beginning to come out or in coming out to their parents. Reading them, a question that can arise is why didn't the person come out earlier? The answer touches on the natural human fear or vulnerability, present in all of us, of being rejected by those we love. It's easy to understand why LGBT people would have this fear when we think back on the environment in which we all grew up in, and in which many of the LGBT people in this book first discovered who they were.

In the past, being LGBT was about being different, other, undesirable, a problem, being bad, sinful, and someone who carried huge stigma. For many years an LGBT identity was synonymous with sexual practices rather than identity. What's really evolved over the last number of years is that people now see it as an identity, not a practice.

In a remarkable speech from the stage of the National Theatre in 2014, Dublin-based drag performer Rory O'Neill, who performs as Panti, cast a cold light on the oppression he continues to feel as a gay man. The online video of the speech has been viewed well over one million times and seems to articulate for many the stress of constantly 'checking myself' to see 'what gave the gay away' in order to avoid verbal or physical harassment or threats. His eloquent speech woke many people up to what the experience of being gay feels like, even in contemporary Ireland. In the book, *Ireland Says Yes*, former President Mary McAleese wrote,

> *...there is more work to be done, for the work of dismantling the entire architecture*

*of homophobia is still not complete. The achievement of marriage equality surely and irrevocably propelled us further along the road. It lifted some of the intolerable burden our gay and lesbian children have to carry.*

Social attitudes have changed in Ireland and had changed prior to the marriage equality referendum. We know from a public attitudes survey in an *LGBTIreland* study that, by and large, there are positive attitudes to LGBT people. This survey was undertaken in 2014. These positive attitudes were confirmed – and built on – in May 2015.

Social attitudes, work environments and college and university environments have changed for the better. Further change is still urgently needed. More people are coming out and at a younger age. The *LGBTIreland* study demonstrated that there has been a hierarchy of progress – gay men are doing better than lesbian women; and both gay men and lesbian women are doing better than bisexual men and women, and LGB people are doing better than trans people.

In the area of mental health, younger people are at higher risk and experiencing more distress than older people – those between twenty-five and fifty-five.

However, primary and secondary school environments have not changed in the same way. Everyone is legally bound to attend school in this country, and the evidence is clear that the negative environment for LGBTI (Lesbian, Gay, Bisexual, Transgender, Intersex) people in school, where half experience bullying, is causing harm to the mental health of young LGBTI people. In fact the *LGBTIreland* study showed that there is a strong statistical link between experiencing LGBTI-related school bullying and depression, anxiety, stress, self-harm, suicidal thoughts and attempted suicide.

This study showed alarming levels of self-harm with 40 per cent of those aged between nineteen and twenty-five having self-harmed, with half of those doing so in the preceding year. The figures were even more startling for those aged between fourteen and eighteen, where just over 50 per cent had self-harmed, with over three-quarters of those doing so in the preceding year. Despite significant social progress, the youngest people are those most likely to have self-harmed, with 60 per cent of those who self-harmed saying that the self harm was at least somewhat related to their LGBTI identity. The study also showed that 70 per cent of the fourteen to eighteen-year-olds had seriously thought of ending their own life and one third had attempted suicide. Clearly the journey to full acceptance of LGBT people is a long way from complete.

In preparing this book I met many people who were prepared to share their stories. It is not easy to tell your inner most feelings to a stranger. On occasions we laughed and joked. On other occasions we shed tears. All those telling their stories had complete freedom to reveal as much or as little as they felt comfortable with. In some cases people originally interviewed for the book asked that their stories should not be included in final publication. I fully understand why. But each of these people, in their own way, has helped contribute an important element to the overall project. Elements of these stories feature in the accompanying play.

The outcome of the May 2015 referendum has seen a dramatic change in people's attitudes to the LGBTI community in Ireland. But my own experience in travelling around the country during the campaign brought one thing home to me very clearly about much more work needs to be done to bring about inclusion. Common to many of the stories is that the process of coming out is never over. Each time someone moves to a new school, a new place of work or meets someone new – the coming out story is always there to be told afresh.

Proceeds from the sale of this book will go to the suicide awareness organisation, *Console*. This was a deliberate choice because in some of the stories, a minority it must be said, people spoke about having suicidal thoughts at some point in their life. Hopefully young people in the future – and, indeed, those who may not be so young – can read the stories of others who have already struggled with their sexual identity and became comfortable within themselves, most often with the love of their families and friends. All of us can learn from those who have gone before. I hope *A Day in May* will be read and enjoyed by the wider community.

The book is dedicated to the 1,201,607 people who voted 'Yes' on 22 May 2015. But, like those who were in the

GPO during the 1916 Rising – which began the process of Ireland gaining its Independence – I have a suspicion that in the years to come, many more people will claim they cast their vote in favour of the 'Yes' in the marriage equality referendum. If that is the case, they are more than welcome to be included in the dedication for this book.

Photo: Karl Hayden

*Enda Morgan and his wife, Audrey married in 1985. They have four children – Rachel, Shane, Emmet & Ellen. After retiring from the banking industry in 2008, Enda founded Blush Wedding Music, which is now one of Ireland's leading wedding ceremony and reception music providers. Enda spoke about his daughter Rachel and her partner, Marion, at the launch of the Yes Equality campaign prior to the referendum in May 2015.*

# Enda

I am here because of my daughter. I've been married for thirty years. I'm a married man with four children. My eldest daughter is Rachel. She's twenty-seven years of age. About five years ago Rachel came out to my wife and myself. It was a very harrowing evening when that happened. Not because Rachel is gay, my eldest brother is also gay. So Rachel knew for a long time I have had a touching point with the gay community.

What was harrowing about that evening was how upset Rachel was when she told us. She was shaking. She was crying uncontrollably. In such a situation it is very difficult to be a parent and to hold your child in your arms. It was very distressing. What distressed me most was that Rachel had bottled this up for a number of years before she spoke to us.

If that was how Rachel felt, then how are other people feeling? What about those people who don't have an understanding parent? That frightened me even more. I asked Rachel about it, and she said, 'Yes Dad, there are many, many people still out there who have not come out to their nearest and dearest. This is why the referendum is so important.'

Rachel had suffered from anxiety and panic attacks for over a year. We couldn't figure out why. But from the day Rachel came out to us this anxiety stopped. She just blossomed and flourished. Now she's happy and confident. She's got her mojo back, and it's fantastic to see.

Two years ago, she met Marion, the love of her life. Rachel and Marion are deeply in love. They come to our home, and what we see is fantastic love. It's the same love that I have for my wife. The love that Rachel and Marion have for each other is the same love as in any heterosexual relationship.

I work as a wedding musician. The first same-sex civil partnership I played at was after Rachel had come out to us, and I found it really, really emotional. We were at the top of the room singing and playing. Kathy and Pauline walked into the room. Love walked into the room. I looked around the room – grannies, granddads, aunts and uncles. Everybody had a wonderful day. And the love that walked into that room is the same love that walks into every wedding that I play at. The same love.

We have to make our children comfortable so they don't have to live with the type of anxiety Rachel experienced. Everybody has a touching point with someone in the LGBT community. It's our LGBT family. Rachel and Marion don't want to go down on their knees and say, 'Will you join me in a civil union?' They want to say, 'Will you marry me?'

*Marion Doherty (L) and Rachel Morgan (R) got engaged in June 2015. The couple – who Enda Morgan spoke about at the start of the marriage equality referendum – will marry in August 2016. Marion is a member of An Garda Síochána. Rachel is Head of Casino at an online gambling start-up.*

# Rachel & Marion

*Rachel:* It was very emotional to watch Dad speaking at the campaign launch. I kind of forgot our story until I heard him telling it again. It was like, wow. It was a pretty emotional speech for me, for Marion, for all of us. I was completely overwhelmed. I had never really heard Dad speak in public before so I had no idea what was going to come out of his mouth. I just knew that he had been asked to do this talk from the perspective of a parent. He was standing up there not caring what anybody in the world thought. I have to say it was one of the most incredible feelings in the world to watch your own father stand up and defend you in front of everybody. And not to care and not to look nervous, just telling the truth. He didn't embellish the story. He just told it as it is. And he didn't hide his or my mother's feelings.

It was around the age of twelve or thirteen that I started to realise that I was a little bit different, without even recognising what that meant or how I was different. But it wasn't until I turned twenty-one that it really hit me like a ton of bricks. It was completely inescapable at that point. But I had always thought to myself that if I'm gay and if somebody asks me, I will deny it. I will marry a man. I will have two and a half children and all the usual stuff. I was only telling Marion the other day how it was so all-consuming. I didn't know one gay person except for my uncle who was abroad. One day I just sat down and googled 'Gay Ireland'. That was my first step. I didn't know what to do or where to look or who to talk to. I came across this website, a forum for Irish gay people, where they talk about TV shows and normal stuff. And that was kind of the start of me realising that I was gay.

At that stage it still absolutely terrified me. Nobody was going to know. Telling Mum and Dad was just not on the agenda. Eventually I met a girl in Galway. She was in exactly the same position as me. We got chatting online about what the hell we were going to do with our lives and about how we couldn't tell anybody. Everything just completely terrified us. We met up and became really great friends. We started going out, getting to know other gay people, and that was how it all began. But I was telling my college friends I was going out with friends from home and telling my home friends that I was going out with friends from college, and my parents thought I was somewhere else. I got myself completely caught up in this unbelievable tangle of lies. There was so much going on in my life and nobody knew about it. I was getting lost in my own lies. Like where did I tell them I was last week, and people were saying, I thought you said you were out with Janey or whoever. I realised I was coming closer and closer to essentially getting caught. And that had a really big effect on my mental health at the time.

I remember I had gone to Galway to meet some friends in the gay community, and I had told everybody else I was somewhere else. When I was driving home from

Galway, I was to go to a friend's birthday party, and I was thinking, 'Where will I tell them I was?' because I had to come up with a whole back story as people will ask what clubs did I go to and what restaurants did I eat in. So I was on the motorway from Galway and I had a huge anxiety attack which I didn't even realise at the time was an anxiety attack. All of a sudden I started feeling really weak and warm. Really strange. My heart was pumping out of my chest. I pulled in on the side of the road and I rang my mother. I said, 'Something is happening. I can't breathe.' Everything was starting to blur. I had a rash and I didn't know what's happening. So I called an ambulance because I was completely convinced that I was dying, and my mother was in Dublin thinking that I am dying on the side of the motorway.

The ambulance arrived and took me to Tullamore hospital. They ran all sorts of tests, and at the end they said, 'You had an absolutely massive anxiety attack.' And I was going, 'You're crazy. I'm not worried about anything. I'm not leaving until you tell me what's wrong, because that's not what happened.' So then I went to my local doctor in Dublin. He asked me a few questions and then he said, 'There are nine signs of anxiety and you have twelve of them.'

At the time I didn't even notice it was happening. I had never really heard of an anxiety attack before. But every day at about nine o'clock in the morning I would start having these kind of heart palpitations. They would happen at the same time every day, and especially when I was driving home from somewhere trying to come up with a lie to cover my tracks.

My parents had no idea what was going on. They were trying to help me but I wouldn't let them because I didn't want to tell them the truth. I ended up in counselling, and I slowly realised that I couldn't live like this forever.

When I eventually sat down with my parents I just couldn't get the words out. I am sure everybody who is gay will agree that actually saying the words 'I am gay' out loud is probably the most difficult thing ever because you are kind of saying it to yourself as well. I think I eventually mimed the words. I couldn't say the words, 'I am gay.' The way my Dad describes when I came out is a bit of a blur to me because I was in such a state of panic. I was a complete basket case, shaking and bawling crying. My parents were absolutely incredible. And after I told them I got to untangle the web of lies I had created. The anxiety just started to go away on its own. And now I'm obviously flying. I met Marion a couple of years ago. We are engaged. Everything is completely different to what it used to be.

*Marion:* I am from a small village in Co. Donegal called Dunloe. I wouldn't say I knew I was gay from the age of twelve. But I would say I knew I was different. I wouldn't have had access like Rachel would have had to social media or the internet. So it was very isolated, and there was absolutely nobody to talk to. As I went through my teenage years I think I realised that, yes, I am definitely gay, and then I was panicking a bit. I used to think that the only way around this was probably to move away. I told one of my close friends at the time, Paddy was his name. And he was brilliant.

I would never have had a boyfriend, but I went through the motions. Went to dances, kissed a couple of boys, just because you had to. The last time I kissed a boy I was about nineteen, and I just thought that's enough of that, you know. I'm not going to pretend anymore. After I finished school I went to Letterkenny. I got in with a nice bunch of friends there. I played sports. I just didn't want to tell them. From listening to banter around changing rooms, I just didn't want to be the lesbian on the team, in case they would push me away. So I kept it to myself.

I applied for a couple of jobs in Dublin, got one, and just bit the bullet and moved down. I still hadn't come out to my family at this stage. So I was twenty-two and my family didn't know. So when I moved to Dublin I remember telling my Mum, and just asking her not to say it to anyone else. I was very nervous. I just sat down at the kitchen table and thought, 'Right, it's now or never.' I remember getting really upset and she was really concerned. She kept saying, 'What's wrong with you?' I couldn't get the words out. It was just a wave of emotion. And then when I got the words out there were floods of tears and apologising. I was like, 'I'm sorry, I'm sorry, you know, I don't want to be like this but I can't help it.' She was very good.

You know, it was a weight off my shoulders but I still didn't want my Dad to know. I wasn't ready for that. But there must have been rumours going around at home because I remember Dad rang me at one stage, and he just said, 'What's this I'm hearing about you being gay? Is that true?' I completely denied it, so I did. And that was definitely the wrong thing to do.

I think I was always a daddy's girl, and I just never wanted to let him down. So when I was confronted by him, I actually felt shame. I thought I was disappointing him. The worst thing I did was to completely deny it and I probably kept up that pretence for another six months. But it just all came to a head and I had to tell him. Looking back now it was crazy, and such a waste of a good seven years that I could have just been myself.

At the start when I joined the Gardaí I kept it from everyone that I was gay, which again was a mistake. The close group of friends I made when I went to Templemore first, I kept it from all of them throughout the two years' training. You don't want to walk in the door of your first station and have them think that you are the gay one or whatever. So it was another hiding thing. It just puts a burden on you, because it's another web of lies that you are creating. But as I built friendships with people I would have confided with one or two here and there. So then eventually everybody knew, and I have never had any difficulty.

Now that I am completely comfortable with myself and I have my confidence. Looking back, it was an unnecessary burden because every time someone found out they were perfectly fine. It was me that created the burden and me that carried it. I didn't lose any friends over it or I didn't have any awkward confrontations or anything like that. Everyone was very accepting and very supportive. So I think it was all just me, it was just the paranoia that I was feeling. Looking back, if I had known that it would have been accepted the way it was I would have come out much sooner. It's the same story we hear all the time, people worry so much and it doesn't end up being nearly as bad as they think it might be.

It's been great now everyone knows. Everyone is delighted now to see me settle with Rachel. The most recent wedding invitation we got had both our names on it, Marion and Rachel. It was actually nice. I liked it. I have never noticed anybody look at us funny in the street although we have had a couple of funny experiences in hotels. I remember about two years ago we stayed at one well-known hotel. We had booked online so when we arrived we went up to reception and the woman behind the counter said, 'I am sorry, miss, but you have booked a double room, do you want me to change it to a twin?' And I said, 'No.' And her eyes just darted from the two of us, you know. And she was like, 'Oh, oh, ok. Sorry.' That happens pretty regularly. I always feel sorry for the person behind the counter because they get really awkward and embarrassed when they shouldn't.

I remember the day we went to look at the venue for our wedding reception. The wedding co-ordinator came over to Rachel and me and she said, 'Which one is the bride?' And we went, 'We both are.' And she was like, 'Oh, of course. That's fabulous.' That's what we find so funny because, of course, normally it's a guy and a girl getting married. So naturally people are going to ask, 'Who is the bride?' We're getting married in August 2016. We're both going to wear dresses. No dickey bows for us. It's still a bit unorthodox, I suppose, so we can kind of make up the rules as we go along. We are suiting ourselves a lot but it's going to be relatively traditional.

*June Hamill is fifty-one years old. She was born and raised and is still living in Cork. 'Out and proud circa 1987' is how she describes herself. She played an active role in the Yes Equality campaign in Cork.*

# June

I was born and raised in Cork. Presentation Sisters educated, primary and secondary school. Brother, sister, mother, father. I'm the eldest child. I'm fifty-one years old. When I was growing up I would have been commonly known as a tomboy. I would play hurling or football with the lads morning, noon and night. I had a mad interest in soccer. People will find it hard to believe now, but that was prior to BBC and Sky, and all we had was *Match of the Day* on a Saturday night. But there was also local soccer. I used to follow Cork Celtic. They were my first team from about seven or eight years of age. I'd go over to Turners Cross, which is about a hundred yards from where I lived. That was my life. If it involved sport I was happy. I didn't have a particular interest in anything else.

When I was like ninteen or twenty people would say, 'Have you a boyfriend? Have you a date?' And I am looking at them, thinking, 'No, what would I be doing with a boyfriend?' And over time, I suppose, I became aware – hang on a minute, there's something going on here. I'm not a bit interested in boys in that sense. Like to me, if they couldn't kick a football or hurl they shouldn't have been on the earth. And, bit by bit, the more I was going out with friends, the more it began to dawn on me that I would have been attracted to women.

But that just didn't fit the norm, or the norm that was my life, and my family's life. But I suppose like so many other people you come to the stage where you know because it becomes so much more of your life. You are denying yourself the thing that everyone at that age is looking for – the fun, the chance of a life together with somebody. Eventually I did something about it. I orchestrated it that I got to talk to somebody who I knew to be gay, on their own. She was so supportive and in a completely non-pressurising way.

This woman said to me like, 'If you ever want to go out there's a bar, Loafers, where people meet on Thursday nights in Cork.' She said, 'Give me a buzz beforehand and I will make sure that you have a friendly face at the door.' I did nothing for a number of weeks but eventually I picked up the phone and went, 'OK, what pub did you say?' From where I lived Loafers was on the left-hand side of the street as I walked towards it. So, of course, I walked on the right-hand side and I walked from one end of the street to the other end and back up and back down, and back up, and then I went home. And I did that on about four different evenings. I was just too scared to go in the front door of the bar. It was like the world and his mother would see me go in. But eventually I did. And I got to be friends with people.

I wasn't out at home. I eventually told my sister, who didn't give a damn. My best friend knew from day one. She's straight and she didn't give a damn either. But no-one else knew. And then I told another friend of mine. So my two closest friends knew. But I said to them if they ever met my mother and she said 'And you were out with June on Thursday night'

– they had to say they were. So Thursday night was the night I would go out but I would use my two closest friends as buffers. And that was the way we dealt with it.

That went on for about three years. It was appalling. Three-quarters of myself was consistently hidden. At work people talked about their weekend, their boyfriends, their girlfriends, their children, where they went, what they saw. And they would say to me, 'June what did you do?' And I would say, 'Ahh, no, I wasn't out at all.' But I would have been out Friday, Saturday and Sunday. Having had a ball but I couldn't find the confidence in myself. I hadn't really come out to myself.

It was an awful strain. I remember having a problem with my ears. So I went to the doctor who couldn't see anything wrong with my ears. They sent me to an ear specialist, and I will always remember the specialist's words. He said, 'You are a very young lady, Ms. Hamill. I don't know what the problem is, but you need to start dealing with it or that won't go away. There's nothing at all wrong with your ears.' It was stress. I suppose it tells you what the body can do when it's not dealing with stuff. I was living a double life, completely a double life.

I eventually met someone, and fell madly in love. That's when things began to slightly change for me. My partner's name was Nuala. I was living at home but I used to stay in her place maybe one or two nights a week. To this day I don't know if I would ever have told my parents. My common sense says I would have done, but I am not sure. My younger brother overheard me on a phone call telling someone I loved them. He told my mother. He was probably only twelve or thirteen at the time. My mother was, 'What?' She asked my sister who said, 'Oh I don't know.' My sister phoned me straight away and said, 'June, there's a problem.'

I remember driving home from work saying, 'Right, if she asks. I'm not denying it.' So I got home. My mother was mashing potatoes. She bawled, crying into the potatoes, and walked off upstairs. I knew it wasn't going to be easy but I had decided in my mind we are having this out now once and for all. So I followed her upstairs. She was sitting on her bed roaring crying.

*'Is it true?'* 'Is what true?' *'You know what.'* 'I don't know.' *'What are you?'*

I was like, say a word, and we will go from there. I think she might have said, that you are actually going out with this Nuala one or whatever, that you are one of them. She didn't say gay or queer – it was like one of them. Because, I suppose, being a child of my generation I sat down, and cried and apologised. 'I'm so sorry. There's nothing I can do about it. I'm so sorry I'm disappointing you.'

When I think of it now. But, at that time, I thought that was the way to handle it. And my Mum was like, 'I can't understand. What did we ever do wrong?'

This went on for about three-quarters of an hour. I actually thought I was going to vomit. It shook me. It shook me to my core. And in the middle of all this, I heard the thump, thump, thump, up the stairs. It was my Dad. And I was waiting for him to come into the bedroom but he never came in. My Mum used to work at night at the time. So we got to a point where she had to go to work. She said we will talk about this again or whatever. And I said, fine. I just remember coming out of the bedroom thinking, 'Oh Jesus, if this is the rest of my life I don't want it.' And my father was standing outside the bedroom door. And I looked at him and I said, 'I'm so sorry.' And I bawled crying again. I mean it was 'I'm going to fall to my knees' stuff. And I always remember he took a step forward wrapped his arms around me, held me up and said, 'You are my daughter, I will always love you.' The whole house was in turmoil now as you can imagine. Mum was gone to work. And I went downstairs. My father was now in the kitchen. He said, 'Do you want me to make you a cup of tea?' And I said, 'No'. I was standing there. I was shaking from head to toe. Still bawling crying, nose running, everything. And he turned around and said, 'Do you want to go to Nuala?' I didn't even know he knew her name. And I said, 'Yeah.'

*Bill Hughes is an award-winning television producer. He lives in Dublin with Gary, a Welshman, his partner for nineteen years.*

# Bill

I'm from Athy in Co. Kildare. Born in 1955. I'm one of thirteen children. I was the loud, over-achieving middle child. My parents were straightforward God-fearing people. My father from Armagh, my mother from Tipperary. So they met in the middle and ended up in Kildare. He came from a Protestant tradition up north. She came from an extremely Catholic republican tradition down south. And so in our house that kind of stuff didn't get talked about because it would only be too contentious. The house was God-fearing, not liberal, but they ended up having to become liberal, as we grew up, because we all had very strong personalities, the kids. We all wanted to go in different directions with life and our expectation of life far exceeded what our parents' expectation of life was. The way we wanted to express ourselves, you know, like my mother famously said to me once, 'Who told you you have an opinion?' And I was like, 'Everybody has an opinion.' She said, 'No, not in this house.'

I always knew. I was always the one that was fascinated by the big entertainment shows on telly. I was a cliché myself. My mother's father, my grandfather, commented once that I walked in a funny way, that I had turned-in feet. I walked like a duck. And he said, you would need to be getting him playing more sport to break him out of that. So my father brought me to boxing lessons. You see a cartoon sometimes of a kangaroo, that people have put boxing gloves on, and the kangaroo is up with the top two little fists just banging. That's what I looked like, I looked ridiculous. I was never going to be a boxer. My brothers were champion hurlers. My brothers were champion footballers. I was good at tennis. My brothers were fantastic runners. I was good on the bike. I was able to do certain things, and I was reasonably fit. But I wasn't butch. I have five sisters, and they had dolls. I was fascinated by the dolls. I was always into drama. I was one of those incurable romantic kids, where everybody falls in love, everybody has a lovely time and I dreamed of what I was going to be like when I grew up, having a wife and children and all that sort of stuff. But then come the age of ten, eleven, twelve I realised 'Well, no, I didn't want a wife.' I wanted a man in my life. But obviously I didn't know I wanted him as a husband. But I wanted a man in my life.

I was always attracted to big powerful men. I was an altar boy and I had a crush on the priest. There was a Christian brother, I had a crush on the Christian brother. There were two teachers in my junior school, I had a crush on them. There were two teachers in my senior school, I had a crush on them. I went away to boarding school. I had endless crushes, you know. So I was Mr Crush, you know, but I was too afraid to do anything about it. I was terrified that I was going to be either beaten up or exposed. That somebody was going to call me something bad, you know, a queer or a faggot. But I had a very sharp wit, I had a very sharp tongue. I would cut the feet from under anybody who said anything smart to me so they would give me a wide berth.

I came out when I was sixteen. And my parents were at the end of a long kitchen table. And there had just been a programme on TV and it was one of those heavy interview programmes, but the subject of the interview was Christopher Isherwood, one of the great writers of the 1930s. And I remember at the end of the interview there were only me and my parents for whatever reason. The interview was about the loneliness of being gay in the 1930s and 40s. And my mother was saying, 'That poor man, that poor man, what an awful thing.' And my father was just saying, 'Yeah, but he was a genius.' And I said, 'What if I was like that?' And they were, 'What do you mean?' My mother was, 'Don't be ridiculous. That's just nonsense. You couldn't be. You are only looking for attention.' My father said he had met lots of men like that on his travels, and the one thing they all had in common was that they were lonely. And he said, 'I hope you never tell me that you are lonely, because I will have failed you.' And that was it.

My mother instantly wanted me to go and see a psychiatrist. To fix me. A friend of hers made an arrangement for me to come to Dublin to see a psychiatrist. This was 1972. I was sixteen. I was a big fella, a good-looking fella. I was playing tennis, I was in great nick. I looked a lot older. So I came to Dublin to the psychiatrist. He was this weedy little man who stank of cigarettes and stale whiskey. I sat down in the chair and he said, 'Now what seems to be the trouble?' And I said, 'I think I'm bisexual.' And he said, 'Don't be ridiculous. Most young guys go through that phase.' I went back the following week, and he made a pass at me. So I thumped him in the face, and I walked out and never went back.

I came to college to UCD. There were dark days. I was pretty much out to most people. But most people didn't really understand it or believe it at that time, because it was kind of a new thing. There was a fantastic character called Gerry McNamara, and Gerry subsequently became a senior scriptwriter in RTÉ and wrote *Nighthawks* and all that sort of stuff. Sadly Gerry got AIDS and died. But in UCD Gerry was a fantastic English student. He would march through the corridors of Belfield in a blue velvet cape, and everybody was, 'Darling' and 'Are we going down to the dram soc?' I remember thinking, 'OK, I'm gay but I'm not that gay.'

I was going through my lumberjack phase. I had long hair. I had a Jesus beard. Check shirts and denims. I looked like a refugee from the Mamas and the Papas. I was having sex with girls. Of course, I was trying to sort of take the heat off myself by being seen with really attractive girls. But all my big crushes were men. Water polo players and rugby players and big fellas, they were my supermodels. I didn't need posters of women on my wall. I just needed a mental image of those guys.

In Dublin in the early 1980s gays would meet on a Saturday afternoon at The Old Bailey pub on Duke Street. It would be a great place to socialise, real fun. But this is a secret society. Everybody within the group was thinking, 'Nobody knows.' Everybody outside on the street doing their shopping didn't know that we are all queers. From about 1983 or 1984 people started to get sick in awful ways. They would get terrible growths on their faces or they would go through a sudden massive weight loss. They would have a terrible cough, and then they would be weak. They would disappear and then they were gone. And you would hear they had died. That was when the whole AIDS thing hit. Nobody knew what it was. People were like, 'What's happening to us? Is this a deliberate thing? Are they trying to wipe out gays?'

People thought they got it from poppers. No, it came from blood, it came from semen, it came from sex. People got very angry about it. And my great friend, Vincent Hanley. I was producing him at that stage. Fab Vinny. Vincent was from Clonmel in Co. Tipperary, and he was the first superstar DJ in Ireland. Not only did he have a career here but he also went to England. He had an extraordinary agent who had three clients: Terry Wogan, Kenny Everett and Vincent Hanley. He had his own show on Capital Radio in London. And he was being offered BBC network shows. But Vincent knew there was something wrong, and he wasn't telling anybody. Instead he was doing MT-USA on RTÉ, and he said I have to be in America more. He was visiting a clinic secretly for treatment. Right up to Vincent's death, he was in denial that it was AIDS. He just kept telling everybody that he was going to get better.

When the word got out that he was very bad, people would come up to me and say, 'How are you, Bill? No symptoms yet?' Vincent and I were friends, we were never lovers. But people said I was going to get it. It was just awful. So when Vincent died because of the false concern of people I decided I'm not going out again. So I didn't go out for three years.

I lost my college peer group to AIDS. I stopped counting after thirty friends, and that's just in Dublin. I could count thirty friends in New York, thirty friends in London, you know, I could count so many people who died in so many parts of the world. I have photographs of dinner parties in my old house on South Circular Road where there were maybe ten of us around the table, and I'm the only one alive. Everybody died of AIDS. I don't know how I didn't get it.

The deaths from AIDS were particularly difficult because the people who were dying of AIDS needed somebody to hold their hand, needed somebody to wipe their forehead, to touch their feet, to just give them ordinary human interaction. And in those days there was so much ignorance that people didn't know if they could actually touch somebody. There was the most frightening weight loss, the most frightening-looking gauntness. People were afraid of those with AIDS. There was nothing to be afraid of but you just couldn't reason with them.

They looked at people who had been their friends, who they had been out partying with six months previously, people who everybody had always said, 'Oh God, isn't he gorgeous?' and then they would be saying, 'Oh, Jesus, he has it and there's nothing left of him.' When they died, the inhumanity, nobody could see them, because they were instantly put into these zip-up body bags that were then sealed. Their coffin was sealed. So nobody got to see them, nobody got to touch them, nobody got to say goodbye properly. It was really horrible.

There was definitely nothing good about being gay in those days. And that's why everybody was so much in awe of David Norris, that he was putting his professional career and his reputation on the line by declaring that he was gay and tackling decriminalisation. What David did was extraordinarily brave, because he put his head above the parapet. Most people didn't. Most people were very happy to not call attention to yourself, you know, don't be so flamboyant. And for every gay that went to The Bailey on a Saturday afternoon there were thousands who wouldn't dare ever be seen out in a public place like that.

These days I see guys holding hands, saying goodbye to each other with a kiss, like its a normal thing to do, a kiss to your beloved. It's not just male/female beloved, it's now female/female beloved and male/male beloved. And it's a beautiful thing. I see people of the same sex holding hands, walking down Grafton Street, Georges Street and Henry Street. And it means something to me. Because it says, 'My God, how far have we come.' In the old days, in the 1980s and 90s, you would have bottles thrown, you would have young thugs jumping up on you on the street, thinking it was funny to whack your head off a wall. So to go down the street now, and to see a simple overt expression of affection, a public display of affection, to see that means everything to me.

Photo: Kate Nolan

*Ben Slimm is twenty-seven years old. He was born in Birmingham but raised in Tralee, Co. Kerry. He is an advocacy worker on behalf of the student movement and has a particular interest in social issues that affect students.*

# Ben

I was born in Birmingham in 1988. My Dad is British and my Mom is Irish. I lived there until I was about four when my parents divorced. So we moved home after a stop-off in Plymouth for a couple of years. I've lived in Tralee in Co. Kerry since I was about seven or eight. I had a little British accent coming into school. And you know hearing the accent I had people wanted to know where I was from. That's the first thing I remember. I didn't want this accent because people identified me as different. Now my accent is completely neutral. I can't explain it at all but I just remember thinking I'm so different to everybody in this class. I just could never find anything in common with them. So I spent a lot of time on my own. I always felt different.

It's very hard to describe because you don't have a word for it when you are young. I never had a word. I just knew in secondary school there was one boy in particular in the class and I really, really liked him. I couldn't understand why I really liked him. But I wanted to be best friends with him and I just wanted him to always be my best friend. Looking back on it now I suppose that was the first real feeling that I might have had a little bit of a crush on this person or maybe romantic feelings towards him. But I was only a child so I didn't understand it.

I suppose the first time I ever heard the word gay was when I was told I was gay in primary school. Faggot was a very,

very popular word then. I think it still is but not to the extent it was then. I would have been in fifth or sixth class. I was involved in a young people's group, a real theatre school. Once a week we would have dance and singing lessons. I loved it. I went to an all-boys school. I had no friends in school but once I was outside school I had loads of friends, and they were all female. I was practising for some show in the Siamsa. My mother wrote a letter to the school to say I had to practise for the show, and could I stay in at lunchbreak to practise. I asked her and she wrote it. So I was practising in school and a couple of the guys came in, typical males, do you know, boys will be boys. I was dancing and they went, 'Oh God, you are such a faggot.' I knew what it meant loosely. And that became a real permanent feature of my life until I came out, the knot in my stomach, not wanting anyone to know.

I would have gone to church to see if that would help. I was in the choir at school. I was an altar boy although we wouldn't have been a real church-going family. I remember when I became an altar boy and my mother saying, 'Why are you doing that?' I thought if I was holy then I wouldn't be gay. I wanted to get married and to have children. That was a big thing in my teens. I wanted to have kids. I remember thinking, 'God, I want to have a family around me, to have kids, and if I'm gay I can never have any of that. So please, God, please, please I'll do anything it takes, just don't make me gay.'

I spent most of my time in school trying to pretend I wasn't someone that I was. So I focused mainly on that rather than actually being interested in class and I suppose the bullies noticed that. I don't think I was bullied from the start because I was gay. I'm quite a loud mouth. I speak out quite a lot. And I think it was identified by other kids in secondary school because I was different to them. I think they knew that I couldn't identify with them. And the reason I couldn't identify with them was because I was gay.

I don't think they directly started bullying me because I was gay. I remember in secondary school 'gay' started to come more and more into the mainstream, and it was more on our televisions. There was a gay relationship in *Coronation Street*. My mother is an avid *Coronation Street* fan, and I remember sitting in the living room the first time there was a gay character and actually being so tense, sweating, a knot in my stomach, being like, 'Oh my God, is she going to look at this and then look at me and realise that I'm that person on the television?' That I'm gay. And being so tense about that. So I think once the bullies made the distinction that I was different because I was gay I think their actions did become about being gay then.

I was beaten up a few times. I remember one day I had to go to the shop for my mother. There were these boys. They had called me fag and queer and that they were going to get me after school. One of them was in my school, and the rest of them were in different schools, but they were going to get me after school for being a fag. It was because I was gay that they wanted to get me. It was a dark winter's evening and I was walking down to the shop. They came out of the estate and they chased me. I got cornered. I was in someone's front garden. There was nowhere for me to go. And they literally beat the living daylights out of me. I was kicked. I was punched. Fag, queer was shouted at me. The lights were on in the house and I remember banging on the front door to get someone to help me. No-one helped me. I had to go to hospital because I had quite a swelling on my head and I had a broken wrist.

I was beaten up more times than I can actually count. I was punched or kicked five or six times, and there must have been hundreds of times that it was verbal abuse. It had quite a profound effect on my mental health. I went through a sustained period of depression. I never attempted to take my own life but I did think about it quite a lot.

I missed school because I couldn't face going in. I would make up any excuse to stay at home which again had an effect on my education. My mental health was not good. Boys never speak about being upset. I remember a few years after I came out to my mother, she said there were times when I was a teenager that she worried that she would wake up and she wouldn't find me alive. And I remember thinking, 'God, I put her through that.' And my first thought was for her and that I allowed that to happen.

I had my first real boyfriend when I was nineteen. I had moved away from home, and I rang my mother to tell her I had met someone. I didn't say I was gay. I just said, 'His name is Russell.' She said she was happy for me, and that she had always known. I couldn't tell my father. I don't know why because he has always been a fantastic Dad to me. Like, my Dad is the world's number one Dad. If I ever need to talk to somebody I can ring my Dad. But I remember saying to my mother, 'I can't tell Dad. You are going to have to tell him.' It was a real disservice to him and I regret that. I should have told him myself. A couple of days after coming out to my mother, the phone rang and it was my Dad. He was in complete shock. He said, 'I never expected it. It's not something I would ever have thought about in a million years.' He said he loved me, and that I was still his son. He said it wasn't the life he would have chosen for me because it was a difficult one but all he wanted was for me to be happy. When he said that eight years ago I remember thinking, 'It is a difficult life and it is going to be more difficult.' But we have more rights now. And I wouldn't change anything in a million years.

Photo: Tristan Hutchinson

*Jenny Hannon (R) is originally from Blanchardstown in Dublin, but has lived in Limerick since 2002. She completed a BA in History and Social Studies at the University of Limerick in 2007. She currently works as a drug and alcohol worker. Jenny and her fiancée, Ann Blake (L), got engaged in 2012.*

# Jenny

I finished my degree in Limerick, got a job, and then I was living out in Killaloe. I felt like I was never going to meet somebody because I was living in a rural place. And that really affected me. I felt very lonely. But I just kept myself very busy, you know. I did a lifesaving course, I joined a football team. I completely over-committed to work and then I realised that I was focusing on what I didn't have as opposed to being thankful and grateful for what I did have. And the minute that happened, and the minute I let that go, I met Ann.

I came out in 2006. I'm thirty-two now. So I kind of came out late. I always had concerns or questions about my sexuality but by the time I actually came out it was because I met somebody. And that gave me the language to be able to articulate what was going on for me. My fiancée Anne, we have been together five and a half years. We got engaged in 2012. So we have been waiting since then to get married.

We worked on the tally at the referendum count in the University of Limerick. The next day Ann was really hung over, and I was sent down to the pharmacy to get Solpadeine. I was totally femmed up, in a dress and everything. So I went down to the pharmacy and I said, 'Can I have a small packet of Solpadeine?' And the pharmacist said, 'Have you used it before?' And I said, 'It's not for me, it's for my partner.' And he goes, 'Has he used it before or has she used

51

it before?' Like, over fucking night. And I was like, 'Yes, she has. Thank you. Cool.' It felt amazing like because for once I didn't have to make a decision or expose myself or have to correct somebody or just pretend I'm straight.

This was something that my Ma said to me. She felt that the day after the referendum if there was a gay person walking down the road, and someone gave that person hassle there's a whole load of people now that will turn around and defend that person, and say to that person, 'You can't treat that person like that.' It's not only one person now because Ireland has decided that homophobia is not OK.

Hopefully we will have a generation now who are coming out and who don't have serious mental issues around their sexuality. I had a suicide attempt when I was young, maybe twelve. I link it to my sexuality, definitely 70 per cent of it, you know. I tried to hang myself. I took the rope from an old-fashioned man's housecoat, a large one, and I tied it to an old built-in wardrobe, a lot of the council houses had them, tied it onto the top of the wardrobe. But the rope snapped. I got a real fright. I was just very lucky that I survived. I had left notes for everybody, saying goodbye and that it wasn't their fault. I just didn't want to live. It was all around that feeling of not belonging, that feeling of feeling misunderstood.

Looking back, it was horrendous. I was out of control and very destructive. I felt like I didn't belong. My life was a lie. I was drinking a huge amount. Like I remember one time in first year in school drinking. I bought a bottle of white wine. I had had a naggin of vodka before it. And I drank the white wine in about five minutes. I got so sick that I burst all the blood vessels around my eyes. I had to go into school the next day like a pink panda because I had vomited up the lining in my stomach. To this day, I love red wine but I can't touch white wine because of that association.

There was a lot of drunken sex even at that very young age. I was very sexualised as a teenager. I was always with boys and I had sex with boys. Anytime I was with any fella I was absolutely off my head. I've never ever been with a fella sober. I was just very lucky I didn't get pregnant or contract a sexually transmitted disease. There was a lot of turmoil, just that feeling of not really belonging. I never made the connection to my sexuality until a bit later.

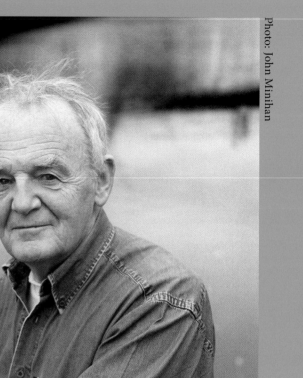

Photo: John Minihan

*In the late 1970s Arthur Leahy was one of the first people in the country to speak on television about being gay. He is a founder of the Cork Gay Community Project and has had a long-term involvement in Cork's Quay Co-operative initiative. He is also a member of the Board of GLEN.*

# Arthur

I did an interview with Áine O'Connor on RTÉ. She was very sympathetic. It was a good interview about my partner and myself at the time. He was an Australian lad. The interview was about our lives as a couple living in Cork. I forget what the programme was called but the reaction was very favourable. It had quite an impact.

I was aware what the reaction of people would be. There was a lot of fear beforehand in my family. Being gay was kind of a taboo subject, you know. Some of my siblings were like, what will the neighbours think or you will never get a job or, you know, the world will fall apart. But I had enough experience to know that that wasn't going to happen. I must say throughout my life I've always had huge confidence in the Irish people and in their sense of fairness. So my mother stepped forward and said, 'Look, I think this interview is great. If he wants to do it, he should do it.' It was a very courageous thing for her to say. I think that's partly to do with the Irish character.

In the 1970s in Ireland there wasn't really a word for being gay. We used to scour the British newspapers to get a sense of what it meant. You would get it sometimes in book reviews. By the age of fourteen I was reading reviews of the most esoteric of books where you would get a mention of it. At that time I would have come across as very confident but that's the nature of young people. There wasn't the same pressure as there is today for younger people to have an identity. Being gay was something that was kind of creeping up on you as a young person, whereas nowadays teenagers have to have a sexual identity. Today there's a huge urgency on young people. I actually think they are under far more pressure than I ever was.

I'm involved with the the Gay and Lesbian Equality Network (GLEN) and there were discussions that maybe the referendum was coming a bit too early. I would have subscribed to that view, in the sense that we should leave civil partnership for another few years. I felt the result could have swung the other way. I was very fearful. I had three responses. There was my head, my heart and my stomach. So I would analyse the campaign through those three responses. Like my head would sometimes say, we are going to win this. Like my heart would say, definitely, we are going to win it. But then my stomach would say, no, we are going to lose it.

And my response changed depending on canvassing on a nightly basis. I remember going down to the smaller towns in west Cork where we were kind of trying to set up hubs, you know, local hubs as part of the campaign. And some of our people were afraid. They said they couldn't do door-to-door canvassing. They were saying, well, maybe we could do a survey. But that changed so quickly. Campaigners got confidence as the feedback from talking to people on the doorsteps was surprisingly positive.

Photo: John Minihan

*Kathryn O'Riordan describes herself as a proud Cork woman, lesbian and mum. Her partner, Anita, and her family and friends are central to her life. She works as an Early Years Professional and sings in Cork's LGBT choir.*

# Kathryn

My mother died when I was twelve. I was absolutely
terrified of upsetting my father as he had been through
so much. He was raising four of us on his own. I was
petrified that I would upset him. That was my main aim
– not to upset him. So I hid everything about my life
from him. I didn't tell him about my friendships. I told
him vague things. It worried me all the time. I came out
when I was about sixteen. It wasn't a popular thing to
do but myself and my friend we are both dykes, and we
kind of had each other which was lovely. But it worried
me all the time. I was frightened of people's reaction. I
was physically afraid. People threw stones at me on the
street. It was really quite a scary time. I had cut my hair
very short so in a way I drew attention to myself. I was
both terrified and brave at the same time. I remember
holding my friend's hand in a pub. An older woman
asked us not to come back because we were too visible.
Many of us at the time were physically frightened. I
admire so much the brave men and women who weren't
frightened. Obviously they were older than us.

It was understood that people could lose their jobs. It
wouldn't be OK for teachers. It wouldn't be OK for nurses,
doctors. There were artists who were quite free and writers
who were fine. But people were worried that the landlord

would find out, you know those kinds of things. It sounds like a lot longer ago than the 1980s but, you know, it wasn't. That's what it was like.

It was very interesting around the referendum. Because a lot of us remembered. I think there is a case of misremembering. My family is really cool now but we have been on a very long journey together. My older sister, when I told her, she cried. My younger sister, when I told her, she cried. They were absolutely horrified. They were really upset for me, and that something might happen to me. They were worried for me and also they were ashamed of me. It's all terribly nice now. We are all very cool. We are all terribly OK with the gay thing now.

I know my sister regrets it now. I think she does. But I wouldn't ever talk to her about it. I would never upset her about it but I was upset at the time. The perception now is that we are a really cool family, and we have always been really cool about this. It's not true. When many of us lesbian and gays talk, we go, 'Yeah. I had that experience too. They weren't cool, do you know.' Last Saturday night, my sister and her husband, my partner and I went to their house, and then my other sister and her husband turned up, and we were all talking about this wine and that wine, and it was lovely. It always is lovely. But we don't talk about twenty years ago and the 1980s, how shit that was.

When I was in the UK in 1997 – and this is a very important part of my story – I adopted a little girl. Because I worked with children, I have always worked with children, I really wanted to be a mum. So adoption was possible there but it was only possible for a single person at the time to adopt. You couldn't be a gay couple. So we went through a very, very, very difficult process. We ended up with a new baby, which was unbelievable for gay couples at the time.

The courts weren't fine about it. We had to go through the formal legal process. It ended up taking three years, because no court would take a decision. So we kept getting moved up the courts and moved up the courts and moved up the courts until we ended up in the Royal Courts of Justice with a very, very prestigious judge having to take the decision. Our daughter is seventeen now. She is fantastic. She's just wonderful. It was the best decision that we ever made. And Jules and myself are very, very close as parents. We are rearing her together even though we don't live together any more. And it's great. We are a very post-modern family.

Photo: Tristan Hutchinson

*Nuala Ward has been an LGBT Human Rights advocate since 1986. She describes herself as a feminist and artist. She is the organiser of the Pride parade in Galway, the longest consecutive Pride parade in Ireland.*

# Nuala

I am from the midlands, from outside Athlone, a little country village called Finnan. I came to Galway for a weekend in 1986 and thought, what the hell am I doing in Athlone? So I stayed here. This has been my home since then. I came out when I was sixteen. But I didn't know I was coming out. I didn't know any of the language. I didn't even know the word 'lesbian'. All I knew is that myself and another sixteen-year-old girl, we were in love, and it felt really good. Everything kind of made sense to me. I was really happy. I thought everyone would be as happy for me, so I told people. I was like, 'Oh you know, I have a girlfriend.'

Then word just spread around Athlone. The town was so small. I hadn't thought it through obviously. I just thought when people understand it will be fine, you know. But it was a rough few years in Athlone. I was beaten up. I was walking near where I lived. It was evening. Something was thrown over my head. I presume it was a jacket. There were male and female voices. I didn't see who it was but they were laughing and obviously having the craic. I was kicked. They were shouting 'lezzie' and 'queer'.

I went to the Garda station, because that's what you do. I told the guard, and he was saying, 'Why do you think they were robbing you?' And I said, 'No, it's because I had a girlfriend.' So he just closed the book and said, 'Well, what do you expect?' I felt more humiliated in that moment than I did when the assault was happening. I didn't know the word homophobia at the time. Like I didn't know anything. I didn't know that I had come out. This was all language I learned years later. But the guard's words really stuck with me.

After the incident with the guard I kind of realised that there were other people like me in Ireland. So I got involved with a group of women, and we did training in Cork and Belfast on the lesbian lines there. Then in 1989 I organised the first Pride parade in Galway. Fifteen people marched that day. We now have the longest running Pride parade in the country.

When we got an invite from Mary Robinson we brought a Connemara candle to burn in the window in the Aras for all the LGBT people who had emigrated because of their sexuality. I worked on the helpline for over ten years. And at Easter and Christmas, and in the summer, we would get calls from people who were home on holidays. We used to have a befriending system for them. A couple of us would meet them because there was nowhere to go in Galway at the time. They hadn't left because of work. It was because they couldn't live here and be themselves. It was either go or die. I think if you can't be yourself and carry on with your life and be respectful of others, then a huge part of you dies.

Photo: Tristan Hutchinson

*Sharon Slater (L) is an author and local historian. Sharon's partner, Susan, is a computer programmer. The couple have been together for ten years, held their civil partnership in 2012 and live in Limerick. Sharon's son, eighteen-year-old Stephen Clancy (R), is a keen amateur actor.*

# Sharon & Stephen

*Sharon:* I've seen people attacked for being gay, and that's not pretty. About three years ago I saw the worst attack. I don't drink but I go out with my friends. There was a drag night in a local pub in Limerick. When I was leaving I rang my partner to come and pick me up. I was waiting outside the front when a kid, he was only nineteen, poor dear, came out. He was only about a hundred metres away from where I was. And these two guys and a girl walked past me. I stepped back as you could tell, you could sense from them. They walked up to him, called him a fucking fag and then they just started beating the crap out of him, kicking his head. His face was destroyed. As soon as they went I went up to him. I ended up covered in his blood. A taxi pulled up and the driver put a bandage on him and then drove away. I had to get the police and an ambulance. It was just horrific.

I came out first when I was sixteen, but it was in Tipperary in the mid-1990s. It was still very Catholic even though I wasn't Catholic. So I went back into the closet at that stage. The reception wasn't great at all. It was very isolating for a long time. When I was seventeen I met someone and I ended up getting pregnant with Stephen, and we got married. Then soon afterwards we had Peter, and not long after that we broke up. Then about ten years later I met Susan, and we've been together since then. I'm now thirty-six. I'm a historian, and a mother. We've got a lovely little neighbourhood where we live. We all say hello. We've got Brazilians living down the road. And there's the lady who's got the granddaughter. Everybody in the neighbourhood has a name. So we are probably the lesbians with the boys. That's probably what they call us.

*Stephen:* I turned eighteen the day the marriage equality legislation was signed into law on 29 August 2015. It was quite a relief that it was passed. The 'No' campaign had been using the issue of children, saying that it was discriminating against us, for it to be passed. I wanted people to know what was actually going on and how children raised by gay couples themselves felt. Just to show how much voting 'No' would be discriminating against us.

I prefer having two women as parents, Susan and Sharon together. I was young when I first learned that they were going out. They met online. I don't see them as any different from any other couple. They are just like any other regular parents. I've always called them by their names. Actually I've jokingly called them mother and Mom and Dad but it's only really been joking. And they've laughed as well except when I call them Ma. They are not fond of that. But I prefer calling them by their names. It would be quite nice to see them get married.

*Rebecca Murphy was born and raised in Cork. She loves baking, roller derby, cats and dogs and swimming in the sea. Rebecca was a member of the Yes Equality Cork Committee.*

# Rebecca

I'm twenty-nine years old, not quite thirty. Not yet. So we will avoid saying that. I have spent my whole life in Cork. Growing up being gay in Cork was very lonely. I suppose I wasn't really aware of any other LGBT people at all really. I don't remember knowing any gay or lesbian adults. When I began to realise I was gay, around the age of twelve or thirteen, I didn't think it was even a possibility. It was something that happened to people in America or on TV or in films, you know. Like there were no lesbians in Ireland. I think it wasn't until I discovered the internet really that I actually began to realise there were other people in Ireland and in Cork who were gay. I started getting in touch through online communities and then eventually getting in touch with actual people. That made a big difference but I suppose in my mid to late teens it was very isolating.

My mother knew that there was something going on, that I was hiding something. And I think she was probably just desperate to figure out what was going on inside her seventeen-year-old's brain really. I used to write loads of poetry as teenagers sometimes do. My mother found a book of my poems. Some were about just this girl I had kind of feelings for. She read this book of poetry which was kind of mortifying really, when you look back at it. The poems were about just being in love as a teenager, sappy kind of romantic love poems. Some were probably a little bit dark as well, just kind of about that loneliness and about feeling isolated.

My mother sat me down. And I knew she had read the book. She was actually very concerned. She was more concerned about the poems that were very dark, and that indicated maybe I was feeling quite down on myself, than she was concerned about the ones that indicated I might be gay. So she sat me down, and she was kind of saying, look, I read this book, and I just started bawling crying. Because I knew she knew that I was gay at that point. And I just clamped my hands over my ears and just thinking, 'I am not ready, I am not ready for this, I am not ready for this.' And I wasn't. I wasn't ready to come out at that point to my parents. Because it's a very scary thing, the idea that your parents might judge you or reject you. And in hindsight I don't know why I ever thought that. Like I often say to people I could probably walk in the door with six heads and they would still be like accepting and supportive. But I think in hindsight it was just a very scary moment, and a very scary kind of experience.

*Ed O'Callaghan, a tailor by trade from Cork, was married for nineteen years when he came out.*

#  Ed

I was married for nineteen years, actually technically I am still married, because we are not divorced. I got married in 1989. I was twenty-four. It was very exciting. And it was something I actually really wanted to do. It wasn't something that I was forced into. It wasn't something that I was made to do. I met my wife, like, we met at fourteen. We used to pal around together. And, you know, over the years a friendship turned into a relationship. We went through periods of, it's all off, it's on, it's all off, it's on. But we got to a stage around eighteen or nineteen when we became a little bit more serious, you know. It was a fun time. It was a good time. And it was a happy time even though, if I am honest about the whole thing, I knew I was gay since about I was fifteen.

I grew up in the Ireland of the 1970s and 1980s. Cork was a very small place. I always call Cork a village, not a town or a city. Everybody kind of knows everybody. For me to be an openly gay teenager would have been a no-no. I hid from myself for an awful long time. I met my future wife when I was fourteen. And I remember at around fifteen or sixteen I told her I thought I might be gay. And in fairness she said, 'Do you need to go and speak to somebody? Do you need to go off to explore, you know, to find out for sure.' And straight away – barriers: 'I went, no, no, no, no. I do not want this. I don't want to be this person.' From then on I just suppressed it. We got engaged at twenty-one. Saved to get married, and got married at twenty-four. Became a dad at twenty-five, and loved it. Really threw myself into it. So the gay thing was never mentioned.

I was so proud of myself that I never once strayed. I never allowed myself to stray. I was forty-three when I had my first sexual encounter with a man. I kept it suppressed that long. It was hard, I suppose. Coming out was a process. I actually didn't even decide to come out. It just happened. I probably was just feeling sorry for myself, that I didn't allow myself to the live the life I should have lived. And, you know, I kind of had a little bit of guilt, and a little bit of resentment.

In January or February 2008 I was on an online chatline. And I was chatting to a guy in London, and we found that we had very similar stories except he wasn't married, but he was living with a girl at the time. And we both knew we shouldn't be here, we should be doing other things. We just chatted and chatted, and that went on for a long time. Then we decided to meet. So in August 2008 I flew over to London. I always remember it was lunchtime on a Friday and I met this guy, and we walked around London just chatting and chatting. There was nothing sexual or anything like that. On the Saturday we actually kissed. And it was the first time I ever kissed a man. I was forty-three. It was just a kiss. But, for me, it was unbelievable.

I was still married. I suppose that's contradicting what I said that I didn't cheat. Maybe I did for two days. Later at home in Cork I was chatting with my wife at the kitchen table. And you know she says, 'What's happening with us?' And I always remember, I got up to flick the kettle, and I was standing, and I just turned and I just said, 'I have something to say.' I actually remember holding onto the kitchen worktop, because my whole body was shaking. I just said, 'I'm gay.' I think that was the very first time I ever said it out loud. And straight away the shaking stopped, everything stopped and I just felt a calmness. It was a very weird, surreal sensation. Naturally enough there was wailing and bailing. But we also chatted. Cried, chatted, cried. But there was no anger.

My mother was not so good with the news. She was thinking of my wife and the kids, and, you know, what's going to happen with them. And I am saying, 'They are going to be fine.' My father blew me away. He was never an overly affectionate man. A wonderful father, certainly, and a great provider, but he was a typical man. As kids if we had a problem, you would go and talk to him and he'd say, 'Speak to your Mum she's better at those kind of things.' But that day when I told them I was gay he just hugged me and told me he loved me, and said 'Regardless, you are my son.'

My kids knew nothing of what was going on at the time. We kind of just kept a front up. I mean they obviously saw that we were upset. My son would have been eighteen and my daughter would have been twelve. They knew there was a strain, that Mum and Dad were having problems. I told my son first that I was gay. And he said, 'I knew, Dad.' That's what he said to me. 'I knew.' And I said, 'What?' He said, 'I've always kind of had a feeling. I knew.' So amazing, brilliant, not a bother. It was never an issue. It never became an issue with me being gay. I think me and his Mum splitting up, I think, that was harder for him. But not the fact that his Dad was gay, which really, really surprised me.

Myself and my wife had decided not to say anything to my daughter, as she was just too young at that stage. We just felt that rather than going and saying to her, 'Look, Mum and Dad are going to split up, and Dad's gay' we decided that when she was old enough to ask the questions, then we would tell her. I was in and out of home. I had initially moved out. But financially it was crucifying. So myself and my wife decided that I should move back in. There was an extra bedroom there. So it was fine. Because we had known each other since we were fourteen we were best friends before we became boyfriend and girlfriend, husband and wife.

My wife always said, that if I was having an affair with a woman she would have probably done something, and fought and stood her corner. But she said, 'I can't compete against a man, if it's a man that you want and a man that you love.' I felt so guilty myself. She should have been really angry. Here she was thinking she was married, had a partner and a soul mate, who would be with her right throughout life and into the twilight years. But that didn't happen for her. I had huge guilt about that. Three years after I came out I actually ended up having a heart attack. And it was the stress of it all. But she has remained an extremely good friend. Even now maybe every second or third day we see each other.

I told my daughter about a year after I came out. She was angry at me because she was last to know. She went, 'Why am I always last to know?' And I always remember saying to her, 'Well we didn't want to say it to you, because we felt that you were too young. And we always felt that if you asked the question then you were mature enough to get the answer.' So I said that we wanted to wait for you to ask the question. She was quite happy with that. She didn't want her school friends to know because she said she would be bullied in school. And I understood that.

When she was fifteen she went to a New Year's Eve sleepover in a friend's. And they were all celebrating. And they were all happy but my daughter got very upset. And the girls were saying, 'What's wrong, what's wrong?' She said, 'You know Mum and Dad are separating' and her friends go, 'Yeah but you know they are grand, they are still best friends.' But she said, 'You don't know the reason why Mum and Dad are separated.' And the friends are saying, 'What's wrong?' So she told them. She goes, 'My Dad's gay.' And her friends, I think she has the best friends in the world, go: 'Yeah. Oh, that's so cute. That's gorgeous. Oh God, your Dad's lovely.' For her it was a great response.

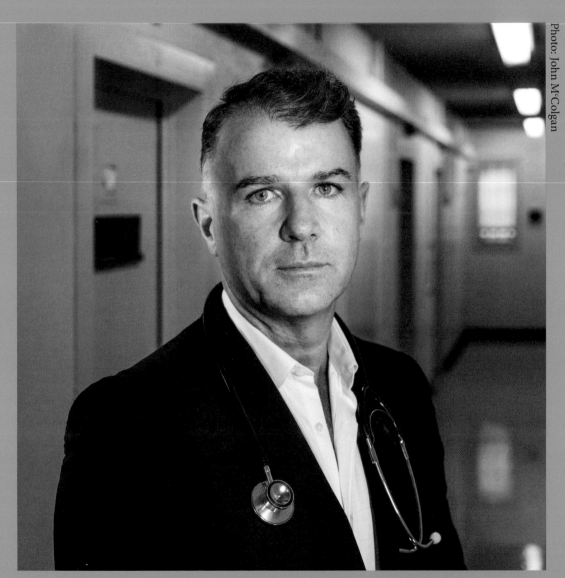

Photo: John M<sup>c</sup>Colgan

*Des Crowley is forty-eight and comes from a farming background in Co. Cork. He has been living and working in Dublin for the last twenty-two years. He's a GP coordinator for the Northside of Dublin overseeing the medical care provided to drug users. He also works in Mountjoy Prison.*

# Des

I'm originally from Cork, from a farming background, a farmer's son. Second eldest in a family of five. I've lived in Dublin for twenty-two years now where I work as a doctor. So Dublin is home. I came out to my family when I was seventeen, and probably to friends and the wider community in my early twenties. When my parents became aware that I was gay, or when I verbalised that I was gay, they sent me to a priest. My parents are of a generation where the church would have been extremely important to them, still is. But I think for the first time in their life probably, they had to deal with a situation that they really didn't have a solution within their own capacity as a couple or as individuals. So that was the context where they organised this meeting with the Franciscan brother. Whether it was about support, or about trying to persuade me not to be gay, I'm not sure exactly what the context was.

The priest asked me to tell him my story which I did. The fact that I had such clarity myself, and I was very rational, he probably was very clear that there wasn't any point in changing me, if that was what he wanted to do. He may well have believed that it was perfectly OK to be gay. Anyway the compromise we decided was that I was to go back to my parents and tell them that I was reconsidering my gayness to alleviate their fears. I never reconsidered but I suppose in their eyes it just took the immediate heat and drama out of the situation. But it cropped up over the intervening three, four, five years and, you know, it would end up just being an argument or a fight in the family, and then things just moved on.

It was a very unhappy time for me. When I reflect on it I think it was the wrong time for me to come out. I went to UCC so I lived at home for my university years. I think that just caused too much difficulty. In some ways it might have been a better scenario had I waited a number of years to come out, or had not lived at home during those years.

It's interesting how life has progressed. My mother was eighty this year [2015]. Myself and my partner were civilly partnered in 2010 and she came to that. She's very close and very friendly with my partner, and vice versa. He's very much part of the family. And she indicated to me that she voted 'Yes' in the referendum. Within my immediate family and the larger family there's been illnesses and death. I think that has contextualised a lot, and how really unimportant sexual orientation is. The bigger picture overtakes, you know.

I work in the addiction services by and large. I'm a GP co-ordinator on the northside of Dublin. I work with another co-ordinator. So basically I would be involved in overseeing the medical care provided to drug users, opioid dependent people in the northside of Dublin. It's a methadone programme. I still do a small bit of general practice, and I work in Mountjoy Prison. I've done that for twenty years. I moved up to Dublin the minute I qualified. I got a job in the Mater, working in infectious diseases. I met so many drug users at the time accessing the services. I just felt that they were being looked after so poorly. They were so sick and the services weren't adequate so I've followed that cause pretty much for twenty plus years now.

I define myself as an AIDS baby. When I became sexually active we knew about HIV, and we were all petrified about it. But at the same time we all wanted to have sex. We were aware of safe sex. I suppose what was so extraordinarily sad at the time was people who had not been aware got infected, young people, young men, across all of the spectrum. The devastation that it caused the gay community, I mean, really the gay community did not recover from it for I would say for ten to fifteen years. What I would call the HIV years literally took up all of gay politics for ten to fifteen years from 1985 to maybe the late 90s. It shut down the discussion about any other gay social issues for that period of time because people were dying. Once the therapy started coming in, where it could be controlled and it was no longer a death sentence, and people started surviving, then you were in a different scenario where you were managing a chronic illness rather than a terminal illness.

But it was devastation. I would have been at between eighty and a hundred funerals over a period of maybe five years. Young men that I could identify with, they weren't that much older than I was. The time from getting ill to dying was a year and a half, two years. It was really a horrendous death. It was very visible, the whole stigma. A lot of people ended up moving to London because of the stigma here, and because the services took a while to develop. A lot of gay men lived a very isolated and lonely life.

The scenarios that people found themselves in where it was clear that a partner was going to die, and then what that would mean in terms of inheritance, and then the whole issue of the body bags, you know how the bodies were dealt with, the whole infectious disease element of it. They didn't allow open coffins. Even long time after it was clear how the infection could be spread there was fear associated with HIV, the use of body bags, closed coffins and all that kind of stuff. It was a huge issue for people, mourning and grieving.

*Philippa Ryder (R) is a civil servant. She has represented Ireland as a committee member of Transgender Europe and has served on the board of TENI, Transgender Equality Network Ireland. Helen (L), Philippa's wife, works in the health service. Philippa is a cycling fanatic and Helen is a doll's house enthusiast. They are very proud parents of Jenny (centre), who is studying History and Politics at Trinity College, Dublin.*

# Philippa, Helen & Jenny

*Philippa:* I was very unhappy and very confused about how I felt. I wasn't quite sure where I fitted in. I just didn't fit in with the rest of the boys at the time. We are talking in my early teens. It was much more comfortable for me to be with girls and listening to their stories and playing with them, and just being in their company. Now saying that, I had a lot of good male friends as well, But I didn't really explore these feelings much because we are talking early 1970s and there was no information around. I coped by staying extremely busy, by throwing myself into projects. I was very involved with the science fiction community. And that consumed me or rather I allowed it to consume me. It took my mind off these deep feelings that I had.

I thought basically nobody else was feeling like this, that I was the only one in the world possibly except maybe David Bowie. But as the feelings got stronger and I discovered a lot of people that were in my position who, as they were growing up and even later in life, would experiment a little bit, whatever dress a little bit, maybe if they were really adventurous they might try a little bit of makeup. But inevitably the guilt would get to them like it did with me. The guilt got to me and I would dump everything. I would put everything into a black bag and

I would put it in the bin and say, 'I'm not doing it again.' But a week later, a month later, I would be doing it again. I was experimenting. I was trying to find out who I was, what these feelings meant, but I had nobody to talk to.

The only person I told was Helen. We were friends for a couple of years and then romance started. I told her back in the early 1980s when we started dating initially. We got married in 1986, and I was exploring a little bit during the early part of our marriage. It was a difficult. It was a strain on the marriage. We had every sort of issue that everybody else has in a marriage – bills, jobs, health – we had all those plus we had this. I tried not to allow it to consume me. But it became more and more difficult.

I think the internet came along at the perfect time for me. Because it was reaching a point where I don't know if I could have coped without finding somebody else to talk to. I was trying to avoid discussing it with Helen because every time I mentioned it to her she would either change the subject or not want to talk about it. I tried not to bring it up because I knew it would be upsetting to her.

But, say, we would be walking through town and we would be passing shop windows. I would be looking at the latest fashions. And I would say, 'Oh that would be nice.' And she would say, 'That wouldn't suit me', meaning her. And I would say, 'Yeah, but for me.' There would be tension and looks, and I would wish I hadn't said anything. But I was desperate to talk to somebody.

I cannot emphasise enough that as time went on I just became so emotional and so frustrated. It was affecting my moods. It was affecting everything about me. It was affecting our marriage. In the mid 1990s Jenny was born. A huge amount of joy. It was an amazing time, a brilliant time and probably for the first year or so it absolutely distracted me. But inevitably the feelings, because they are so innate, so central to my core, they resurfaced. And even stronger than before.

Literally, from about 1982, or thereabouts, until 1998 – so we are talking sixteen years – the only person in the world who knew about me was Helen. When the internet came along I was talking to people online. And to cut a long story short, I started to meet one or two people. I couldn't believe there were other people in Dublin, one in particular who stayed a friend over the past fifteen years she invited me up to her house. She allowed me dress, just be myself, And that was just wonderful. I always told Helen what I was going to do. And as time went on, Helen became more and more accepting. It was difficult for her, of course.

I made my first appointment with Loughlinstown Hospital in 2005 and started on the medical route to full transition. I was pushing the boundaries. I was wearing a tiny bit of makeup, a little bit of lip gloss, a little bit of perfume, just little hints, maybe feminine shoes, I might wear those. Sometimes I would wear tights under my trousers. You know it was all just the little hints. One guy in work did comment on the tights one day. And I wasn't prepared at that point. And I said, 'Oh they are just thin socks.' But I was on the journey, I was very much on the journey. Everything did get easier. I was pushing the boundaries in work. I was letting people see.

In about 2008 I had a chat with my personnel manager at work, who was extremely supportive. Basically what I did was I took my colleagues out for coffee and cake, and I told them. I took them out in bunches, maybe five at a time. Some of them had begun to question but nobody knew the full story. And I said, 'Look, pretty soon I'm going to be coming in as Philippa. This is who I am and it's been a difficult path.' I didn't want any major surprises. I did find that the women in the office were delighted, they embraced me, whereas the guys found it difficult. Some of them, not all of them, found it difficult. Because suddenly they didn't feel comfortable around me, because somebody that they had known for twenty years or more was going to be presenting as female. And how were they supposed to cope with me? How were they supposed to address me? They weren't sure.

Before you go for surgery, you need to make sure that you can cope with living full-time in your preferred gender. It's normally a two-year test. So in 2009 on my birthday, I got my deed poll where I officially changed my name. And I went to work on my birthday in a skirt, heels, makeup, everything. I was delighted with the reaction. I answered my first phone call as Philippa and very quickly it just settled down into a normal routine. This real-life test lasted for two years, and in 2011 I went to London for surgery. Everything went brilliant. It was a life-changing experience, exactly what I wanted. It was painful, uncomfortable, but it didn't matter as it was what I wanted. And from then I've been basically just living life as Philippa.

We've had a very normal marriage, two women living together married. We are a lot more comfortable now than we were. Once I went full-time it became a lot easier, because we could both see that the world wasn't going to fall in. That, you know, we weren't going to lose jobs, lose friends. But we gained ten times more. And once we realised that Jenny was on board, she was so supportive and so amazing, that just solidified our relationship. And it changed from a typical heterosexual marriage to a lesbian marriage basically. We are happy, and we just get on with our day-to-day life, bills, housework and the underlying love is there and it's wonderful. I could not have done what I did without the two of them.

***Helen:*** Secrecy was difficult. Having to hide things, not knowing what was going to happen, the uncertainty of it. Philippa has talked about me being brave going through with it with her. How much that is inertia and not wanting things to change and hoping that things will go back the way they were I don't know. I will say that Philippa many times said, 'Look, I can stop this. I can stop it.' But I knew she couldn't. I knew it would just send her batty if she had to remain in a male persona for too long. Was it difficult? Yes, it was. We were laughing the other night, saying as she got more feminine I seemed to butch up to compensate. And she goes, 'I'm the butch lesbian in the situation.' It got to a point where basically I had to get over myself. I either had to go and support her or we would lose everything. I just thought, 'I don't want to lose her. I don't want to lose what we have got. I didn't want to be alone with Jenny.' I think one of the defining moments for me was when some of the Transgender Europe people were across for a meeting in Dublin. Philippa asked me to go and meet them, and we went out for a meal. These were great people.

I do remember one holiday we were going to Madeira. Philippa's mother was coming with us. I think it was the day before, Philippa decided to get her ears pierced. Oh, good grief, I was furious at her, absolutely furious. I said, 'What if your mother sees this?' Philippa was still in her male persona, but very feminine. She said, 'Well I can get these little studs which are clear plastic, and she won't notice it.' Except they didn't have any. She had these bright pink diamante studs in her ears. I'm going, 'No, no, no… no.' We ended up bringing bits of fishing wire to try and keep the holes open. I spent half of that holiday fuming for going that extra mile. It was almost impossible to cope with that. But these are the silly things we look back on, but they were big milestones for Philippa and big milestones for me and Jenny.

I know it's difficult. I lost some things, and I gained others. I lost the husband, the normal husband, normal situation, normal family, I lost that. But opening it out, I saw that there was so many other different types of relationships and you don't have to be defined by the normal. The love is still there, the hand-holding, the kissing, and I just got to a point where I said, well forget about everybody else's opinion, I don't want to leave this relationship. We are still a couple. We still have Jenny. We still have our home, we still have our life. We have had days. There's been times when both of us thought about splitting up and divorcing but they were never at the same time. If they had ever landed at the same time it could have happened, which is actually what Jenny never wanted. So it could have happened. But the way friends reacted, and my family reacted, to Philippa's transition was great.

My family worried for me. I was a heterosexual woman who is now in a same-sex relationship. And they just want to know that I'm happy, that my life with Philippa is fulfilling in every respect. And they have seen that now. That I wasn't forced into anything, that I wasn't pushed into anything. And they were very open and very accepting and have been. And the neighbours next door were great when it came to marriage equality. After the referendum we got a card and flowers from them. Congratulations. So that was great.

*Jenny:* I'm their daughter. Philippa is Pippa, and Mum is Mum. I remember not being able to sleep, things like that, because I noticed that Pippa was out a lot. Things were tense in the house. I had been really worried. The main thing was that I thought that Pippa was gay and that my parents would obviously be splitting up. That was the big worry I had. I'm so close to both my parents, and the idea of being separate from either of them was really awful.

So I remember being really worried about that, and I said it to Mum, 'Are you guys going to be splitting up?' She said, 'No. We are still going to be a family, we are still going to be together.' That was great. The details didn't matter so much anymore. And so when the transition happened, and I found out, it just made more sense to me, and while I didn't tell people as such, at least I knew myself what was going on.

My best friend will never forgive me for not just telling her. She was at the house, and Pippa came home from work, very female. But in my head it wasn't particularly female, it was androgynous. And my friend said, 'Oh, your Mum's home.' And I went, 'No, that's my Dad.' And she went, 'Ok.' I didn't address it with her for another six months. And when I finally told her, she was like, 'Oh, my God, thank you for explaining, I was so confused.' She was really supportive. She helped me tell the rest of our friend group as it came out.

All my friends would know them as Helen and Pippa. There are some who were there for the transition, but now that I'm in college, I just say 'I've two mums.' They only know that it's a trans situation and if anyone wants to pry any further they can. But they rarely do, because, you know, it's not that big a deal to most people. One of my friend's brothers was told the full situation. He had been warned, it's Philippa and it's Helen. And you're not to say anything rude. My friend and her bother had been at the airport coming back from a holiday with their family, and my parents were there. My friend's brother was just so confused. And he asked her afterwards, 'Which one is it?' My friend texted me, 'This is hilarious.'

Photo: John Minihan

*John Paul Calnan is fifty-two years old. He married Dominic in San Francisco in 2008 after twenty years together. John Paul played a major role in the marriage equality referendum in Cork.*

# John Paul

There were a couple of occasions when I told people I was gay and they reacted very, very badly. All my immediate family were really good. But when the decriminalisation law was passed in 1993 my partner, Dominic, and I did a newspaper interview with a lot of other people. They took photographs of all the people but they subsequently decided to use one photograph, a photograph of me and Dominic.

When the article came out I got a phone call from an aunt. She rang me at work and basically fucked me down the phone for not thinking of her and for going public – 'and now everybody knows', that kind of reaction. She said she never wanted to see me again, and slammed down the phone. I was twenty-eight or twenty-nine at that stage, and I was in a much better place then to deal with that type of reaction. I spoke with my brother, 'Let me tell you what auntie so and so has done.' Today that woman is grand, you know, and she's been grand for years. She has matured a lot. She's in her seventies now. And she apologised to me. It was at her brother's funeral. She told me I was always her favourite, and that's partly why it was so hard for her. She put her hand on my cheek and told me that.

I came out when I was twenty-one. I had a couple of relationships. I was twenty-six when I met Dominic. We fell head over heels in love, and we moved in together five months later. We were together for twenty years, just shy of twenty years. We got married in California in 2008. We had booked a holiday, and our friend Pat said he would join us. We went for three weeks. Pat joined us for the middle week. And when we were there the California Supreme Court changed the law on same-sex marriage. So I proposed to Dominic, and I booked the wedding online. Pat was our witness, and we got married there. That was amazing. It was really, really lovely. We knew coming back to Ireland that it was literally just a piece of paper. We knew that when civil partnership would come in here we would convert or we would register our marriage, and that we would have a party. But that didn't happen. Dominic died a year later. That was extremely difficult.

Dominic took his own life. I found him. And I didn't know, I didn't expect it. Of course, I didn't expect it. Nobody did. He wrote me the most beautiful but tragic note. I say beautiful because he told me how he felt about me and how much I meant to him. And why he was doing this and why he was so unhappy. I have asked myself why so many times. I don't have a simple answer. The reason he gave was very simple, when you read the note, that it was just about work. He was very unhappy at work. And I remember over and over and over again thinking nobody commits suicide because they are unhappy in their job. But then looking back over the previous year, and looking for clues and all that – and in some ways you kind of think in retrospect that the clues were all there, you know. He had developed anxiety. He was a bad sleeper, insomnia. He worried too much about things, and I think there was a huge amount in his past.

He had a brilliant relationship with his mother and his four sisters. He was the eldest. But he had a very difficult relationship with his father. His father was a troubled alcoholic, and his parents split up when he was about fifteen. But I think part of the thing was that he needed to prove himself. He needed to be the strong member in his family, needed to protect his mother and his sisters, and he did that very well. He was very very good to them. But I think partly around the whole area of his job, he felt that he had reached a cul-de-sac, and he needed to be all the time going further. And I think that brought up a lot of things for him, about how he felt about himself. I have talked with his mother about that. I think she agrees that so much of it was coming from his very early years as a child and as a teenager.

The night after Dominic died, and the night I found him, when I came into the house and into the kitchen. On the table was the note. His wedding ring was sitting on top of the note. He never took it off. He wore it the whole time. And it was sitting on top of the note. I put it on almost straight away. And I have kept it on all the time. I miss Dominic hugely. Like, all the time.

When we got married we did it for ourselves. It did add an extra, I don't know, a kind of status or depth or something to the relationship. That was really nice, to be able to get married, like your siblings had got married.

Dominic died in 2009. Civil partnership came in, I think, the following year. But civil partnership began for existing relationships that existed from that day. Dominic's death certificate, under marital status, says that he died single. But everybody knows that Dominic and I were a married couple. We were very content and happy in our relationship.

I did everything I could to change the death certificate. I spoke with the coroner. I spoke with the Equality Authority. I rang the Department of Justice. Saying, like you know, I'm married. I have the paper to prove it. But nobody could do anything about it. The way the Equality Authority put it was you have to have a law in place that you can challenge and, in this case, there is nothing to challenge. The coroner actually held off issuing the death certificate. He said, 'You come back to me whenever but all I can do is issue it until I am directed to do otherwise.'

I'm wondering again, now that marriage is open to everyone, would I be able to register my foreign marriage, like anybody else? My sister was married in the US. She subsequently divorced. But when she came back she just registered her marriage. What we got [with the referendum] in May was absolutely huge. But this would just be for me. It would be really special, just to have that officially stamped. Because Dominic was a married man when he died.

*Garry Hynes founded the Druid Theatre Company in 1975 and was its Artistic Director from 1975 to 1991 and again from 1995 to date. She was Artistic Director of the Abbey Theatre, Dublin from 1991 to 1994. Garry has received numerous awards for her direction, including a Tony Award for* The Beauty Queen of Leenane.

# Garry

I was born in Ballaghadereen, Co. Roscommon, which is my mother's native town. My father was headmaster of the VEC. They got married in 1952. I was the first child. We were a family of six. I went to the Dominicans secondary school in Galway. And then went to university in Galway for four years. In the summer of my teacher training, I got together with Marie Mullen, and eventually Mick Lally, who was a teacher in Tuam Tech, and we founded Druid. When Mick decided to give up the teaching and look for a year of absence he had to go to my father who was his boss. So it was really quite funny.

My sexuality was not something that would have bothered me very much until probably my early teenage years. And then it was really more about feeling there was something slightly different. It would have been something that was in the back of my head. So I had to all intents and purposes very straight teenage years. I went to hops, dances, went out with fellas, had the usual heartbreaks if he didn't fancy you and delight if he did.

I sort of really continued that until college, and then began to be more certain about the fact that there was something different. The extent of that difference was something I couldn't judge though. Whether it was that I responded to both men and women or I responded to women alone. Up to the time I left college I had had a few relationships with women. It was quite private. And then gradually in the early years of Druid, I would say that the majority of people who knew me privately would have known that I was gay.

I didn't tell my parents. I made a very conscious decision when I was in my early thirties to come out. I began to feel incredibly wrong leading the life of a private gay person. As far as I was concerned it was nobody else's business but my own. From a journalist's point of view I would simply answer what I will still answer to a large extent, you know, I don't talk about my private life. It's been made a little bit difficult, given the fact that my civil partnership, a photograph appeared on the front page of the *Irish Times* which was a complete accident and not anticipated. I mean there were reasons for privacy. People would say, are you married? No, I'm not. Have you children? No, I don't. Now, if they want to ask further question, they can ask it. But actually when it comes right down to it I don't believe it's anybody's business.

When I began a relationship with a woman, it was there for everybody to see as far as I was concerned, and at that point I told my siblings. It was difficult in the usual way. But, to be honest, even if they had turned around and sort of taken a stick and beaten me from here to Timbuktu I still wouldn't care. In fact, they didn't, they responded with their usual sort of irony. The last person, because she was living in America at the time, I told was my sister. She is thirteen years younger than me, but she always treats me like I'm the younger sister, and she's the older, more sensible one. I said, 'I've got something to tell you.' And she said, 'What is it?' And I said, 'You know, I'm gay, I'm coming out as gay.' And she just went, 'Oh Jesus Christ, Garry.'

And I said, 'What's wrong?' And she said, 'I thought you were going to say you were pregnant. Oh, Christ, thank God.' Which was kind of nice. And my brother had the same reaction.

It was my own issue anyway, but yes if any of them had any severe difficulty, that would have caused me a lot of heartbreak. It wouldn't have changed anything. But it would have because I'm very close to my family, always have been. I suppose I was deciding about this all my life really. I was going to live and be what I am which is a gay woman. And looking back on it, I wish I'd done it earlier. I realise how much a function of the times I am. I'm sixty-two years old. I've gone from secrecy and exclusion to openness and embrace. But I have seen it all. I do remember conversations when people would talk about gay people, or queer people, or whatever, you know, where somebody would say, 'Oh, my God, I mean whatever about guys, how can women do it together?' All those kind of things that were very, very hurtful. Especially when the people talking like that were people that you liked and knew and somehow respected. Yes, very hurtful, very hurtful.

You are not telling the story of how you live if how you live is being kept a secret from certain groups of people. I mean I was in a long relationship for almost fifteen years with a woman prior to this relationship. I never actually told my parents. But when discussing it with my siblings, it was felt that they knew, and that this was the way it was. I will never forget a family occasion. I think it was one of my parents' anniversaries and the whole clan gathered. The photographer we brought in to do the family photographs kept finding that apart from the children there was an extra woman, and no man to match up.

And she kept trying to work out the math of how, 'No, you can't stand together. We have to have a man there.' And I said, 'We want to stand together.' She was so thick. 'Oh, no, no, no. I can't do that, I can't do that.' And eventually my father cut in and said, 'They are being photographed together.' She just heard his voice, and suddenly dropped everything. And it was a great moment for me because my father was acknowledging, he knew exactly what was going on, and he was acknowledging that we were a couple.

I suppose what I regret probably is coming out as late as I did. If I went to college ten years later I would have come out in college, which is where these things usually happen. You are getting away from home, you are getting away from your parents, you are able to determine things about yourself. I suppose maybe it's not just the times. I am a private person. And making my sexuality the subject of a public journey didn't feel right to me. But it was a pity, but, you know, theatre, that's what took over my life. And I put everything into that and look at the rewards I have gotten from that. So you know, you can't have regrets but if I did have a regret it would be that. I should have come out earlier and to hell with it, you know. But it's easy to say that from the distance with age and maturity.

I remember when I would discover openly gay women, whom I could respect and admire, it was part of the process that I went through in learning to accept. And maybe it's not as important now, it's so accepted. But it certainly was incredibly important when I was younger. The people that I mix with, whether it's in my circle here in my neighbourhood where I live, the greater theatre community of Dublin, Galway and my friends in New York, and I probably think that the percentage of my friends that are gay probably represents the percentage of anybody's you know. Because obviously your first great friendships, when you work in the theatre is in the theatre itself. I was very aware when I was making plays, I was very aware of the fact that part of my hidden identity was actually affecting my response to certain plays, was enriching some of my approach to work in some way. That tension actually helped. And it was a way for me of dealing with it.

The marriage referendum was hugely important. It's fantastic for me. I mean Martha and I deliberately decided to go forward with our civil partnership, even though we knew it was beginning to be likely. And I said, we know it's likely to be passed, but we are going to go ahead with the civil partnership now, because I don't want to wait for an election. In the Panti video, the scenes where he's back in Ballinrobe with his mother and father, I mean all of these things are doing such a huge job at saying, it's normal, this is normal. But I still think when you are going through the process of discovering it for yourself, and discovering what the implications of it are and discovering how you are going to deal with it, I think everybody will still have to go through that. Perhaps it will be easier and it won't be as horrifyingly terrifying as it might have been for me. I know it was miles easier for me. But it still wasn't easy. And I still don't think it will be easy – easier – but still not easy. The fact of the matter is that no matter how accepted it is, you are and always will be part of a minority. And being part of a minority, it's different. Regardless of the amount of acceptance, it's different.

Photo: Tristan Hutchinson

*Steven Sharpe is a twenty-eight-year-old singer songwriter from Tipperary town. He is from a family of seven and now lives and works in Galway city. His band is called Steven Sharpe and the Broke Straight Boys.*

# Steven

I told my friends that I was gay when I was sixteen. But it was always one at a time when I was drunk. I would be like, 'Oh by the way I am gay but you can't tell anyone.' It was so annoying, because I kept doing it instead of just going to everyone at once, 'By the way I am gay, if everyone is cool with it that's awesome. Let's continue to be friends.' But I just kept coming out when I was drunk, like with my Mum. I was eighteen, and it was the first Christmas I could drink. My sister bought me a bottle of vodka, which I made very short work of. I had been an atheist from the age of sixteen but my mother was trying to get me to go to mass. She was saying, 'Why are you an atheist, why don't you like going to mass?' It was such an ordeal. So I said, 'Because I am gay.' She freaked out.

I was really upset that she was upset, because my Mum is pretty cool. She wasn't so much, 'I don't like gay people' but 'life is hard enough, and now you are gay on top of it. It's a really lonely life.' It took her a long time to get over it. She was always, 'Well, why don't you just try dating girls' and I would respond, 'Why don't you try dating a woman, changing your entire sexuality and show me how easy it is.'

I didn't tell my Dad at first. He is a very devout religious man, very GAA, a soccer-playing Irish dude. He was always a bit annoyed that I was such a wimpy kid. He was always tried to get me into football and his way of doing that was plastering my room with Chelsea posters. So I just developed a crush on Roberto di Matteo.

I came out to my Dad when I was twenty-one. I had fallen head over heels in love with a guy, and I was like this is a part of my life that I should tell people about. So I told my Dad in a fit of like, 'I need to… I have something to tell you.' I was shaking. We were in the car. So I said it. And he was, 'Oh, thank Christ. I thought you were going to say you have AIDS or something.' He said he always knew I was gay from when I was a seven-year-old. I was running around in a batman outfit chasing other fellas. He said, 'You are my son, I love you, it's not a problem.' He took it best out of everyone.

I knew I was gay for a very long time and I never opened my mouth. I am so pissed from feeling so bad for so many years, and just hating myself in such a massive way, just really hating myself. I know my parents loved me. I know my family were there for me. I know I had friends. So it wasn't all bad. But I didn't eat. I kind of hurt myself that way. I started to smoke. I hurt myself that way. I started to drink and I started hurting myself that way. There was one occasion where I was standing on my bedroom window ledge, only two flights up, and thinking if I flip I will crack my neck. And then remembering a guy that my Dad worked with fell off a ladder, cracked his neck and ended up paralysed for the rest of his life. And then I thought, if I fuck this up, I won't even get another chance to do it, because I will be paralysed so best not.

But I didn't see a way out. I didn't see a situation. This was to do with my homosexuality. It had to do with everything that was wrong with me. Why wasn't I like everyone else? Diversity wasn't celebrated in Tipperary town in 2004 or

2005 or 2006. I felt worthless, and when you are fourteen and raised completely insanely Catholic, when I realised I was a faggot, I am going to hell regardless if I commit suicide. So I was sitting on a window ledge going, 'I could do this.' As a fourteen-year-old. But then I got into bed and cried.

Until recently I used to perform under a different name because I didn't want people finding out or saying, 'Steven Sharpe, this fabulous queen.' And then I just went, 'Fuck it. This is who I am.' So I now say I am gay with a handshake. I don't come out to people anymore. I am sick of constantly coming out. Like, you start a job and you have to drop hints to let people know that you are gay in case it might be an issue.

I sometimes perform in dresses. My Dad won't come to gigs when I am wearing dresses. He can't stand to see me in a dress. He came to my album launch and there is actually a song about him, 'Who's the man?' Its about how I came out to him, and the questions he asked me. The type of questions straight people ask me about being gay. Like, when did you know? What did your friends say? When was your first kiss? How did you know the first guy you kissed was gay? Do you go to gay bars? All these questions. Do you like Diana Ross? It's like, of course, I like Diana Ross.

I knocked on doors for one day during the referendum campaign. But the first time I went to a door and it was a 'No' I got so upset I couldn't do it anymore. I wasn't strong enough. So I did what I always do. I wrote songs about it and did loads of gigs. It was kind of preaching to the converted but I am very proud of the country. Watching those pictures at Dublin airport like broke my heart. I was so delighted.

Photo: Tristan Hutchinson

*Gary Ridge is thirty-two and a qualified marine scientist. He was recently awarded the title 'Mr Gay Galway' and volunteers for Amach, an LGBT community group in Galway.*

# Gary

I was in the local gay bar in Galway with a friend of mine. We just stopped for a drink. There was a competition on that night for 'Mr Gay Galway'. Someone came up to me and said, 'Oh we would like to nominate you as one of the contestants.' I had no preparation. No idea it was even going on. But I said, 'Sure why not.' There were a few rounds of questions and they whittled us down round by round. One thing led to another and I ended up winning the title of 'Mr Gay Galway' 2015.

I was always quite shy. It's only in recent years that I started to come out of my shell a bit more. But ever since the 'Mr Gay Galway' competition, and being awarded that title, I kind of tried to take part in as many different things as I could. I was never really an active or a visible member of the gay community before. But now with this title, I kind of felt a responsibility to put myself out there a bit more and just help in different ways.

I didn't really have any gay friends at all growing up. I didn't really have anyone that I could relate to. And for years I was in denial of my sexuality. I had the odd girlfriend throughout my twenties. I just didn't want to acknowledge my sexuality. I was just afraid, especially because of my background, a conservative upbringing, and Catholic upbringing. My parents were always quite cagey about homosexual stories on the television, the radio, in the media.

I would never lie outright and say, 'No, I am not gay.' But at the same time I was living a lie. I was lying to myself first of all. I knew I would have to tell my parents at some stage, because I told my brother on my thirtieth birthday. I was like, I will tell them when I feel the time is right. But it took me a while to eventually work up the courage. What happened was, I was actually going to the Dublin Pride Festival. I was just attending it with a few friends. And I decided to walk the parade. They filmed part of the parade and there was a news item on the following day, and I was on the camera briefly, for about maybe three seconds. My parents had seen that news item on the television. So when I got back from Dublin my parents approached me. My Dad said, 'You are gay, are you?' And I said, 'Yeah, I am.' I just had to. So we just sat down and had a long emotional talk.

Photo: Tristan Hutchinson

*Sharon Nolan is twenty-four years old and lives in Galway. She identifies as bisexual or queer. She is a passionate feminist and played an active part in the marriage equality referendum.*

# Sharon

I'm twenty-four years old and I'm from Roscommon. I'm currently managing a costume shop in Galway. So that's my life at the moment. I am an openly bisexual woman. I was very heavily involved with our local 'Yes Equality' campaign down in Galway. And very, very slightly in Roscommon. Most representations of bisexuality see it as very promiscuous and something that's overly sexualised. So with the image that bisexuality unfortunately has it kind of gets left behind within LGBT culture. I can think of ways it's been shown on TV, it's usually the one character who has an overtly sexual nature.

One of my favourite TV shows when I was growing up was *House* and there was a character, Thirteen, and she was bisexual. And when she had relationships most focus was on, is she going to be with a man? Is she going to be with a woman? Now we could have ladies kissing ladies on telly, because everyone likes that. But I think that doesn't really fit into the happy family image that a lot of the organisations were trying to show for LGBT families.

The first friend I came out to was in a Bebo message. We were talking online late one night, and I was like, 'I might be a little bit bisexual.' And that was the first time I came out, and it was just such a relief. I think the second time I came out was in Leaving Cert. It was one of those days in school when it was really getting me down. One of my friends noticed. So we went into the bathroom to have a goss and to catch up. And I ended up saying it to her as well. She gave me a big hug. She said she didn't care but maybe we would keep to between ourselves, just in case anyone else cared. She just didn't want me to get hurt, and that was grand.

I basically tore myself apart for the sake of the referendum in Galway. I canvassed once in Roscommon but it went so badly so I didn't go again. They didn't want to hear anything. So that was that. I just left the leaflets and I went back to canvassing in Galway. Actually that week I had been asked by 'Yes Equality' in Roscommon if I would speak at their launch in Castlerea. And I had like got my speech written and everything else.

I was a little bit scared because it was the first time I was going to be so openly on show. They had all the local papers there and everything. But I was like, this could be the time to do that. Some of the abuse I got on doorsteps, I got told by a woman in her late nineties that I was only like an animal, and I was just fit for the slaughterhouse. This was just because I was canvassing for 'Yes Equality'. We got run off another man's property because Jesus didn't nail himself to the cross for the queers to go around and run the place and defy the word of God. All this sort of horrible stuff.

Photo: Karl Hayden

*Eamon Farrell (L) is a Director at The National Performing Arts School for almost twenty-five years. He has been married to Steven Mannion Farrell (R) for seven years, having married in Canada in 2009. Steven is an artist whose collectors include celebrities and politicians on both sides of the Atlantic.*

# Eamon & Steven

*Eamon:* I have owned a performing arts school for the last twenty-two years. I grew up in Castleknock. I'm the eldest of four kids, two girls, two boys. I liked school academically, but I was very badly bullied in school. I went to a pretty tough Christian Brothers school in Synge Street which now looking back on it was very unfair of my parents really to send me there, because it wasn't local. The people who I went to school with weren't my type of people. I suppose this is the wrong way to say it, but they had very different upbringings to the upbringing I had. And they never in their lives had seen anything like me.

I was very gentle. I suppose if you wanted to categorise it people would say I was very effeminate. But I actually just think I was a gentle young fella, who didn't fight, had nothing tough about him or rough about him. And I was thrown into the middle of this very rough environment in a Christian Brothers school in the inner city in Dublin.

I never felt that I was the same as everybody else. I've never had a girlfriend, never kissed a girl. Absolutely no interest to me. I suppose when I was about eleven I wanted to marry this boy in my class. I knew it absolutely had nothing to do with sex, or nothing to do with kissing or nothing to do with anything like that. It was a marriage that I wanted. I wanted to marry him, two suits going up into the church. Honest to God, at eleven. My Action Men used to live together in my sister's Sindy house. It was so normal to me, that I never really thought that I was different. Because I wasn't different for me, I was different for other people. But I certainly wasn't different for me.

I suppose by the time I was twelve I wasn't really able to keep in the fact that I fancied these guys. And my way always of dealing with my sexuality was to be on the attack. Never fought with anyone. I never threw a punch or anything. But I've a very sharp tongue and I'm very quick-witted, and so I could turn a fight around like that. But I would still get a hiding every so often. I was being bullied and the world was really crap to me at that stage in my life. The worst thing was this thing called wedgies. Do you remember wedgies? They would pull your underpants. Once I had to go into casualty afterwards, because my balls were so black and blue. So that kind of stuff used to go on. They used to push me around or stick my head down the jacks a couple of times. You know it was full on. It was crap. It was really crap.

I never came out. I told people within about the first ten seconds of meeting them. I think up until the age of nineteen I didn't say a sentence without the word gay in it. I was kind of like very politically active in relation to my sexuality at the time. Because I really believed that there was nothing different about me. I always had this thing, and I still have this thing, and I had it during the referendum as well, if you can meet me or if you can meet someone who is gay, or if your sister comes out as gay, your whole world will change. And you will no longer have any of those fears. The biggest problem with the people who were involved in the 'No' side was they didn't know gay people. They said they did, but they didn't. They didn't have gay people in their lives every day. So this is what I did with people, I said, in the first sentence, 'I'm gay, now deal with it.' I was very lucky. Because I never struggled with my sexuality.

I think the referendum was incredible. There's a lot more to do but I think it just opened the door to what needs to be done in a secular Irish society. We got married six years ago. In Canada. It's now recognised in Ireland. It feels fantastic. But honestly, the whole marriage referendum thing for us was so different for other people because we felt married from day one, you know. We got married on 12 June 2009 in Vancouver. From that day we felt married. So we were fighting to have our marriage recognised as much as we were fighting to have marriage introduced. We wanted it recognised.

*Steven:* I think Ireland was changing. We wouldn't have passed the referendum if we weren't at a certain point. I canvassed extensively around our area and the reactions on the doorsteps were incredible. Not all the reactions of course. There were a few that weren't amazing. One woman in Terenure told me she was voting 'No'. An elderly woman. She was very nice really even though she was voting 'No'. And she said, 'I hope it doesn't affect you.' And I said, 'Well it does. If you are going to vote "No" what I would say to you is, maybe don't go out and vote. Because it's not something that's going to affect you.' And we left it at that. I mean she was fine, she wasn't antagonistic, there wasn't an argument at the doorstep.

I'm a visual artist. I grew up in Tallaght. I had a great childhood, a great upbringing. Sex education wasn't great in school, growing up we didn't really know much about anything to be honest. But when I started to realise, maybe at fourteen or fifteen, maybe a bit younger. I mean I always remember an experience I had when we were in The Hague over in Holland. My aunts and uncles live over in Holland so we travel over quite a bit. My Mum and Dad were still together, so I guess I was probably around ten. And we were in a bar and there was a very famous poster up on the ceiling actually of a guy's torso. A black and white poster of a guy's torso and a woman's hands kind of coming across it.

I remember looking at the poster and I made a comment about it. My aunt said, 'Oh, you shouldn't be looking at that.' And I said, 'Well why shouldn't I be looking at it, you know, I'm a guy.' My memory is that I found the guy's torso appealing, I suppose. And that's probably the earliest that I noticed that I was attracted to guys but I didn't really know what it was I suppose at that age. But it stood out to me as an attractive image.

Photo: Tristan Hutchinson

*Caroline Stewart was born in Limerick but lived in Tipperary for thirty-five years. She moved back to Limerick two years ago and says she wishes she had transitioned sooner to be the true woman she is today.*

# Caroline

I realised something wasn't right at three years of age. I didn't know what it was but I knew back then that things just weren't right. When my mother wasn't around I used to be trying on clothes and things like that. But clothes are not the most important part, they are only part of the identity of a transperson. It's about being who you are, being able to be who you are and feeling the way you are. It was only when I hit puberty, eleven or twelve years of age, that I knew. Am I a drag queen, or am I a transvestite, a cross-dresser or what? But it wasn't just that. It was the way I used to dance, the way I used to walk, everything. I knew there was something missing inside of me. I knew that from a very early age.

I've gone through so much torture and everything. All my life I've tried to hide away in a box. It's been so sad, a jail without walls, without bars. An invisible jail which you are in, but you can't get out of. It's the most horrifying situation. You know, I had a breakdown at fourteen years of age, a mental breakdown. I was discovering who I was, and then not being able to be who I am. I was a top A student in school up to that but then I lost interest in everything. I tried to conform a small bit with my family, by taking up male sports like rugby, soccer and hurling. But I was just going through the motions for their sake, not for my own sake. I felt for a long time that I was living my family's life, not my own life. Then one Sunday night I came out. It was 18 January 2014 when I came out and I told my family.

I went to my parents' house to tell them. I saw their reactions of shock. I just turned around and walked out the door. My mother started roaring this and that. She called me a paedophile. She said, 'You are worse than a paedophile.' That's what her term was to me. She called me everything in the world. That was very hurtful. And then a few days later I started getting letters from my father threatening me. And that really, really upset me. I have an older brother who did the same. So I had no other option but to contact the guards. Don't get me wrong, my father was a fantastic father to us. He provided for us all the way, a hard-working man. But the way he behaved, I couldn't go out for about three weeks because I was afraid. I was looking over my shoulder in case they were going to come after me. I eventually got the courage to go to the Gardaí. There was two lady Gardaí and they were very nice. They read the letter that my father had written, and they said, they'd never seen a threating letter like it. He kind of threatened to kill me in that letter.

The Gardaí went up to the house. My father was so embarrassed, and he said he was very sorry. The Gardaí turned around and they said to him that he was saying 'sorry' to the wrong person: 'You should be saying sorry to your child. You know, at the end of the day you brought the child into this world.' I don't talk to them now. My mother always kind of knew. If there was a fashion programme on the television, she used never ask my three sisters, she would always ask me about the dresses or whatever. So she knew something. But maybe she thought that I was a cross-dresser or something, but nothing as deep as being transgender.

I'm proud of who I am, I love who I am. But, do you know, it's been a rollercoaster. All my life has been a rollercoaster. But now I'm feeling that the stormy waters have calmed in my life. I was born in a male body but I've got female feelings and a female soul inside myself. I'm on hormone replacement therapy. I'm on testosterone blockers, which is an injection into the tummy, and everything is going good so far. I go to Loughlinstown Hospital in Dublin to my endocrinologist and he is very, very supportive. All the staff there are lovely. In April last year I put through my deed poll for my name change. My birth certificate is after being cleared as well. I also go for counselling. It is a hundred per cent worth it. I would rather a week as the woman I am than the rest of my life a male. Trans to me is being born a woman in a man's body. But with transition I want the outside to replicate what the inside is. I'm a woman, and I'm being true to the woman I am.

Now that I'm on hormone replacement therapy I'm in the happiest place I've ever been in my life. I feel like I'm floating on a cloud. It's wonderful. But I keep in touch with reality all the time. And I'm very mindful of things but I'm happy so far with the journey I'm going on. The surgery is done in London. You have to be on hormone replacement therapy for between four and five years to get everything working, and for the blocker injections to lower your testosterone levels.

I'm very excited but I have to keep in the moment as much as I can. I've a partner and she's very supportive. Do you know, I couldn't ask for a nicer partner in my life. She's bisexual. She's a very private person, keeps to herself but she's very kind and supportive of me. She says when she met me the first night I was all dolled up, and she fell in love with a woman. 'That's who I fell in love with, it was a woman,' she says because, 'You are definitely a female soul.'

*Will Keane is a project manager who has been involved in the promotion of LGBT rights and is a former board member of Dublin Pride. He has recently moved home to Roscommon to take over the family farm.*

# Will

I was born in Roscommon, moved to Dublin when I was about twenty-five and moved home last year at the age of thirty-five. I was never particularly out when I was in Roscommon but was when I went to Dublin. It was a kind of an awakening in a sense. And when I moved back home to Roscommon, there were various reasons for getting involved in the 'Yes' Equality. But one of the main reasons was, if I wasn't that person who went to Dublin I would probably still be in the closet. Not wanting to sound like a nominee for the Mr World competition, but I wanted to do it for people who didn't leave the county, who weren't so confident. I wanted us to run a visible campaign in Roscommon and to get a 'Yes' vote.

We went to a canvassing workshop. Most of the people involved with 'Yes Equality' had never canvassed before in their life. We were told never go canvassing on our own. But we were at a point in Roscommon where we had a very small amount of canvassers, and time was ticking. So I went to this estate, a very friendly estate. I knew it was a friendly estate. I had friends there. My intention was doing an hour, getting a hundred houses done, and let's say the way the campaign was going that was sixty more 'Yes' votes. So I put on my t-shirt and went knocking on doors.

There was positive feedback at most of the doors that I went to. But because I was on my own every door I went to was like coming out to people again and again. And because they were strangers you didn't know what to expect. It was like exposing yourself, and I don't mean that in a sexual way, I mean exposing yourself like a nerve. It was terrifying. I got about three-quarters of the way through the estate and I ran back to my car, and I just started crying. I ripped off my t-shirt but because I had the pin in under the t-shirt I ripped everything off. And that's when it became real to me – I am not just doing this because everyone is doing it, I am doing it because it's a deeply personal issue. It matters to me. But it also subconsciously has a huge effect on me. And going to doors and coming out again and again, why should we do it?

There were highlights and lowlights of the whole campaign. But that was definitely the lowlight. It just drove home to me how important this was. I have friends who are as gay as Christmas. I don't mean they are camp, they are just de facto gay. They don't go to Pride. They don't see it as their thing. And that's absolutely fine. I would have never assumed that they would go canvassing. And there they were, posting on Facebook, canvassing a hundred houses a night. This was a deeply personal and emotive issue for so many people. And for people that I would never have expected it from. There will never be a referendum like it again.

I had the same spiel at every door I went to. Basically it went:

> *My name is Will Keane. I live on the Portrunny Road. You know that there's a vote coming up at the end of the month. I hope you will vote 'Yes', and I am here to answer any questions that you have.*

That was the approach that I took. I said that I was gay. Some people had no problem. The people that were the hardest to deal with weren't the 'No' side, weren't the religious people. When I say religious I am talking about hardliners. They were great fun because we would actually speak, backwards and forwards. And we would have mutual respect for each other but we knew their opinion wasn't going to change. The toughest people to deal with were the apathetic people. It's not for me or whatever. I'd say, 'It's an important issue. It's ten per cent of the population asking you to see them as equal.'

*Kathleen Sharkey is originally from Tory Island in Co. Donegal. She is a daily mass-goer. She campaigned, along with her son Noel, for a 'Yes' vote in the referendum.*

# Kathleen

I originally come from Tory Island but I left Tory when I was ten years of age. My family moved to Falcarragh and I went to school there. I come from a family of seven. After we moved my brother Anton went to college in Derry. He studied there for about five years. He actually got married to a very nice girl from Rathmullen. I never thought for a minute that Anton was gay. Never dawned on me. But the day he got married he was crying away when he was doing his speech. And somebody says to me – my mother, I think it was, God rest her soul – she said to me, 'Why is he crying?' And I said, 'He is just happy, that's all.' Never thought for a minute. That was thirteen or fourteen years ago.

Anton and wife seemed very happy. But then Anton took sick with depression. I couldn't figure it out because he was a very happy boy, full of life. But he got very sick. He had a nervous breakdown and he had to be hospitalised. He was still married at this time. I went to see him in hospital. We all did. We were very worried about him. He was in there for about four weeks. I went to see him nearly every second day, and eventually after treatment he started to come around to the Anton we knew. I went one day and he said to me, 'Kathleen, I have something to tell you.' I didn't know what he was going to say, but I knew it was important. When he said, 'Kathleen, I'm gay', I just lost my speech, to be honest with you. But I just turned around and I said, 'Well Anton, I will always love you, but you will need to talk about it.' He said, 'That's my problem, Kathleen, that's why I'm sick because I'm holding it back for so long, and I don't know how people are going to take it if I tell them.'

It didn't matter to me whether he was, black or white or whatever. I told him I would always love him because we were all God's children and I was sure so Mum and Dad and the rest of the family would feel the same. His marriage ended. And she was a lovely girl. I think he did the right thing getting his secret off his chest.

I went with him to Mum and Dad's house when he told them. We were in the kitchen. I'll always remember Mum was peeling spuds at the sink. Dad was sitting at the fire beside the range. Anton told them that his marriage had broken up and why. I don't think they knew what to say. Anton looked at me with a look, help me out. So I just made a joke of it. As long as he was happy that was the main thing.

And that was it. It was never mentioned in the house anymore. Anton was always welcomed at home, and when he met his partner, Gerry, he was very good to my Mum and Dad. They lived together in Letterkenny. Gerry was a very nice man. When Mum took very sick, she was in hospital a long time, and if Anton wasn't there, you know Gerry would be there. But after ten years Anton and Gerry broke up. Anton really took this very, very bad. He tried to take his own life, an overdose. I got a phone call to go straight to Letterkenny hospital.

They didn't think he was going to make it. So I stayed beside his bed praying for him with the rosary beads. And I heard a coughing and it was him, he had his eyes open but he couldn't speak because of the tubes. He was crying. I was so glad to see him.

He stayed in hospital for a couple of weeks. Then he went back home to his house in Letterkenny. He actually met somebody from Derry. I know it wasn't going too well with Paddy, because Anton was drinking. He was never a lad to drink. But Paddy wasn't keeping well, and then he took his own life. I had never met Paddy. When Anton phoned me to tell me Paddy was dead my heart went out to him. It was very hard. After the funeral I was kind of worried about Anton. He booked a holiday, a foreign holiday. The day after the funeral he went away. I said to him, 'I need you to text me every day to let me know that you are alright.' He was away for a week.

Anton was just sick and then he started staying in the house, he locked the door, he wouldn't let nobody in. He died from an overdose. He must have taken a lot that time. We waked him for three days. I have never seen as many people in my life. I couldn't believe that he had so many friends. They came from Dublin, from all over. We didn't know them, but they knew Anton. Some of them gay and some of them straight. Everybody was so nice. They said he was one in a million.

He left a note. He said that he was sorry that he was leaving us this way but that he couldn't cope any more with his life, that he had enough. I think his struggles with being gay took a lot out of him. It might have killed him in the end. Growing up Anton was a very happy boy. He was my pride and joy.

I have four boys and two girls. Noel would be my oldest, he's twenty-seven, he's actually studying medicine in Edinburgh. He's thinking about specialising in heart surgery. Noel is a great young fella. They are all my pride and joy, each and every one of them. But Noel had a bit of a hard time like because I knew from an early age that he was gay. I don't know why I knew, but I did. But I remember when I found out first – I suppose because I knew what Anton had gone through in his life – I remember going to the doctor. Noel was three at this stage, and I said to my local doctor, 'I think Noel is gay.' I don't know what it was but I knew, I just knew. The only thing that I was worried about was that Noel would get hurt. I could see that he was being treated differently by people as he grew up.

There are so many gay people here in Donegal. Some are afraid to tell people, and it's not fair. That's why I stood up with Noel in the referendum. All I want is for my son to be happy and to live a normal life and be accepted in the community like everybody else. I canvassed every day. I went out putting leaflets in doors every night. Myself and Noel, we went out together canvassing. Noel flew back from Edinburgh nearly every week to organise the local campaign. Mother and son. Mother and gay son. And friends. So many people went out canvassing. Some doors we were turned away but it didn't make any difference to me. I knocked on every door.

I was at one door, and I met a young lady with a young family. She said to me, 'Well I was all for this "Yes" vote but the parish priest in a sermon said differently and now I don't know what to do.' But when this lady came home her wee girl – it was very funny, listen to this – her wee girl just said, 'Oh Mum, sure the priest always says, we all must love one another.' The wee girl was only seven years of age. And I said 'Give her the vote.' I told her, 'I will be voting "Yes" for my son and for, God rest him, Anton, and all the other gay young people out there. I just want to see them happy in life, because that's what it is about at the end of the day.' There's nobody perfect in this world. I go to Mass seven days a week, but I'm not a saint. I pray every day, maybe in the morning, rosary last thing at night. And the first thing I do when I open my eyes in the morning, before I get out of bed, I thank God for another day and tell him to look after my kids.

*Noel Sharkey (L), with his partner Dr Kevin J. Browne (R), is a pharmacist who went on to study medicine. He had no previous experience with political campaigning but was compelled to take the lead in 'Yes Equality Donegal' when it was reported by the media that Donegal would almost certainly vote 'No'. In the referendum Donegal voted 'Yes'.*

# Noel

Mum had six kids born within ten years. I'm the eldest. It was a busy house, a noisy house. Dad worked away from home from time to time as a fisherman and also on building sites in the UK. So we spent a lot of time with mum in our younger years. I think my earliest memories about sexuality, or me maybe slightly being a wee bit different, were that I had taken a big interest in Irish dancing very early on. It wasn't a thing that boys did around home.

I don't know why that was. But I think I felt safer in the company of girls rather than other guys when I was younger. I wasn't really comfortable with playing football, or you know hanging around with the boys or anything like that. But I was very comfortable with female company and I took up Irish dancing at the age of seven. And despite getting a hard time for doing Irish dancing from other lads, I loved it.

Then when I went into my teens I started to realise that maybe, you know, maybe I liked boys more than I liked girls. I was quite certain quite early on. So that presented me the challenge of, is this something that I'm going to act upon in the future or is it something that I should repress and keep out of my life? And despite having these feelings, perhaps I should never act on them and I need to get rid of them. So in my teens I carried on with the Irish dancing, and I loved that although I was still getting a hard time from certain people at school about, you know, being a sissy.

It was difficult at the time, because it was something I would have experienced every day. It was quite subtle at times. It would be walking down the corridor and a few lads would snigger at you. And you would hear maybe something like, oh that's the guy that does Irish dancing or, you know, that's the gay guy or something like that. And then one or two individuals who were even more bold would kind of shoulder you in the corridor or really go out of their way to intimidate.

I would have felt quite intimidated but I think I took solace in the fact that despite, I suppose, being bullied I was never seen as an outcast, in the sense of the wider circle at school. I had a lot of friends. They were just predominantly female. They were my support network. And then I was busy with the Irish dancing and the Irish music, and I loved that. I got to travel quite a bit with that as well. It got me out of Donegal to see other parts. I was really focused on my studies, which I think was another way of dealing with it as well. My studies were me thinking, this is my ticket out of here. If I do well at school, I can go to university, I can go wherever I want in the world.

I didn't actually tell my parents until I was twenty-one. But they knew well. So it didn't come as a surprise or a shock. I went through a denial stage in my mid-teens. I was like, no, I'm not, I can't be gay. Even if I know that's what I am, I have to get that out of me. I prayed a lot then because my family is very religious. I would pray every night that I would wake up the next morning and that I wouldn't be gay. And then that stopped. I don't know why it stopped. Maybe there was a process then of maybe more acceptance, or actually thinking, well this is the way it's going to be. And then I think I went into more of a contemplative stage of, well you know what am I going to do with my life now? Everything is grand now. I have ten to fifteen incredibly good friends from Donegal. We have been friends since we were four or five. We have an online chat group and we talk every day. And despite me wanting to run away from Donegal and wanting to keep my distance that friendship has stayed strong.

Photo: Kate Nolan

*Oein DeBhairduin is an activist from a traveller background who works on LGBT issues. He is a manager of an education and employment centre and is a founding member of LGBT Pavee. He lives in Dublin with his partner, Dan.*

# Oein

I was in school one day and on the ground I found an invitation to someone's birthday party that had been on a few days before. I picked the invitation up and I asked about it. They actually had a birthday party. Children in the class had been invited but I hadn't. And I asked why, and the boy said it was because his mother didn't like travellers. That was the first time I had that kind of reaction. I think that set a very strong trend in my life of being silent about who you are.

I started having an awareness of liking my own gender around about the age of twelve. I can't actually remember most of it. I think part of me has kind of blocked that out in that transition and confusion. When I was fifteen I told my sister. I told her on 10 May. I remember because it was the day after her birthday. She's a little bit older than me. My family wouldn't be highly associated with drink but I remember that she must have had one or two drinks because she was very jolly. I brought it up, and we had this really awkward chat. She kissed me on the forehead and said, 'That's fine. Let's go shopping.'

The next day I was expecting something, nothing happened. The day after I expected something, nothing happened. Then about three months later we were in her car, and this guy passed in his car and she said, 'Oh. I heard he's a queer.' And then she went, 'Sorry, sorry, sorry, sorry.' That was the first reference so I knew that she actually had recalled it. A couple of years ago she told me that she genuinely thought my coming out was a dream. That's why she had never said anything to me. No-one really talked about it after that. In the family it's now a known thing but no-one discusses it at all. You know a lot of things like the referendum, or my partner, Dan who I'm with for eight years now, are not topics for discussion in any way, sense or form.

When I was eighteen I told my mother. The first day she took it very well. But her response was like, don't tell your father, don't tell your brothers, don't tell anybody. I genuinely think that she was, even now, she's trying to be protective. But that actually petrified me, the idea of not telling anybody, and then, of course, she went and told my father. My mother was very quiet about it. But about a month later I came home and I was in some discussion about something and I did this with my fingers – I made bunny rabbits. I think she associated that with being very feminine, and she did not take that well. I remember standing in the kitchen and she was hitting a wall, telling me to be a man, do you know. That absolutely messed with me, messed with my head.

I very much love my parents, and I do not doubt in any way my parents love me. But I think the message that was communicated to me was that this isn't something that men do. I think that from my mother's point of view she was trying to mind me. But from my point of view, it was very much, you don't belong here. And when myself and Dan got together, I went to visit her and she actually told me to move to Dublin. But being told to go leave Tuam wasn't just go to Dublin. It was very much, like, leave your family, leave your friends, leave your sense of the community, just like, go away, go to somewhere people don't know you.

I try to get home probably once every two months, maybe every six weeks. But I have never been back in Tuam without someone saying something to me, like they might call out queer, faggot, do you know. And these are not like youths. These are grown, intelligent people who have that reaction of, you are not welcome.

I think I have been invited to three weddings like since I was a teenager. With Dan, the other half, the father met him casually once when I was still living in Tuam, and the brother met him casually. My sister has never met him. And my mother has never even discussed him, and we would talk quite regularly. So it's just that sense of you can't bring the topic up, it is totally avoided. Part of me very much wants to be a part of the family, the way everyone else is a part of the family, but people aren't as willing.

My parents had planned a future for me. So when I told them I'm not going to do their future, they lost a part of the person they thought I was. But that person was never real anyways. They would have been happier if I went along and got married. But I know I would have been absolutely miserable because that is not a life I ever wanted to live. I love my family. But there's that distance, that silence, and it's very deafening.

Photo: John Minihan

*Mícheál Ó Ríordáin is a barman with a strong passion for equality issues. He's been the Cork Regional Coordinator with Shoutout since 2013 and was a committee member of Yes Equality Cork.*

# Micheál

I'm twenty-five years old, from Kilnamartyra, west of Macroom. It is a nice, little tight-knit community. Growing up there was lovely. We had a small farm. I only came out at nineteen after knowing for years and staying in the closet, and never kind of venturing to have any type of relationship for fear someone would find out. It was like having a double life. If the lads in school were on about girls I would just nod away and smile and go, 'yeah, yeah, yeah. She's a fine bird like.' I would play along. Nobody would assume I was gay unless I told them. The first initial coming out that I did was to two close friends. And they were speechless, literally like, jaws almost on the floor. It hadn't even crossed their minds ever. But everything was fine. My worst fears didn't happen. Everyone who I came out to was amazing.

When I said that nobody ever thought I was gay, maybe my mother had an inkling. Mothers always do. It was funny, I came out to both my parents in the car. Separately. My mother was driving into Macroom, and she kind of said it in a roundabout way. Kind of out of nowhere. She brought it up like, saying, 'whenever you settle down, no matter who it might be, I hope you will be happy.' She said it in a gender neutral way. And I was like, 'yeah, Mom, if I do settle down it will be with a man.' And she's like, 'Oh I was thinking that alright.'

I had initially came out to my sister as being not straight, as being something else. I knew she would be fine. She's got gay friends. And she was like, just go out and figure it out, and come back to me when you want. Then over the course of that summer I told my closest friends. Then after my mother I was driving out from Macroom with my Dad. And he goes, like very seriously, 'Mike, do you have something to tell me?' He had obviously heard it through the grapevine. And I was like, 'Oh, eh, yeah, I suppose you have heard that I'm gay.' And he said, 'there's been talk of that alright. But it makes no difference, you are still my son and I still love you. And once you're happy, you are fine.' And I was like, 'Sound. Fine. That's sound.' It was incredibly straightforward.

My mother was having dinner with some of her friends. They have a Come Dine With Me kind of thing, where they go around to each other's houses. And they were talking about their kids, and how they are looking forward to being grandparents. And Mom goes, 'Oh yeah, I can't wait for Mike to have kids.' And one of the women was like, 'What? Sure Mike's gay. He can't have kids.' And Mom was like, 'That doesn't mean he can't have kids. Like he can adopt, he can surrogate. Gay people have kids now.' And her friends were like, 'Oh yeah, I suppose. Yeah, yeah, yeah.' Its about just breaking down these tiny little barriers when they just kind of pop up. My Mom's amazing at doing that. Like at Pride in Cork. I was organising marriage equality's presence at Pride. So asked her did she want to come and march in Pride. And she was like, 'Yeah, sure. Why not.' So I had Mom at Pride with me.

Photo: John M<sup>c</sup>Colgan

*Lora Bolger (L) is from Wexford and Gillian McKenna (R) is from Dublin. They met eight years ago while living in Dublin. They entered into a civil partnership in 2013. Now living in Wexford they campaigned in the marriage equality referendum. They got married in November 2015.*

# Lora & Gillian

*Lora:* I'm Lora Bolger. I'm forty-four. I'm from Enniscorthy in Wexford. I work as a garda.

*Gillian:* I'm Gillian McKenna. And I'm thirty-three. I'm from Clondalkin in Dublin. I now live in Enniscorthy in Wexford.

*Lora:* We've been together for about seven years, and in a civil partnership for two.

*Gillian:* I come from a family of two brothers and a sister. We are all very close now but growing up I was a moody teenager. I didn't know what was wrong with me and myself and my sister killed each other half the time. Looking back on it now I think a lot of it was because I was gay. I didn't know what was going on with myself and I probably just took my anger and frustration out on the people that were closest to me.

*Lora:* Growing up there was myself and my sister. We moved around a good bit, but it was all in Wexford. I went to three different primary schools. And I went to an all-girls secondary school. Looking back now I was, I suppose, a depressed teenager for want of a better word. Looking back it's kind of like, how did I not know I was gay? I suppose I just wasn't happy. I didn't really know what it was. I had no clue. I mean gay wasn't even something that would have entered my head. I didn't know any gay people. But looking back it was very obvious.

**Gillian:** After I left college I went to the Canaries to work for a year with a friend, and a friend that I had met through her, a guy who was gay. He used always to say to her, 'Gillian's gay, you know.' And my friend would be like, 'Leave her alone, she's not, you know.' She told me what he said. And I said, 'I'm not, jeeny mackers.' I think I was still very much in denial to myself. One night we were out dancing, and another friend who I didn't know was gay joined us. And we had a few drinks and she went to kiss me, and I nearly had an absolute heart attack. I said, 'What are you doing?' A few years later when I rang her to tell her that I was gay, she was like, 'I knew that.' And I said, 'What?' And she was like, 'Come on, Gillian. Like Jesus. The Canaries, do you remember?'

**Lora:** I went off and joined the Gardaí in Templemore. I ended up dating a guy. A lovely, lovely guy. But absolute madness. And then we got engaged. So then I was like, 'Ok. I have to tell him something.' I had to be honest with this man. So I told him I had had a relationship with a girl in college, you know just kind of throwing that in there, and seeing. He was really cool about it initially. But then everyone he met he wanted to know, 'Was it her? Have you ever been with her?' He was a guard too. I kind of then started to realise it was madness. Much as I really cared about him, and I did love him, but I knew when it came down to it, I was never really meant to be with guys. I just had to tell him. So we sat down and I just said, 'Look, I'm really sorry. I really do love you but this is not really meant to be.' I don't remember exactly what he said, but I know I did hurt him. But a few years later when I got involved with the LGBT support group within the Gardaí when he found out, he called me up and wished me well. I would never say a bad word about him, he's an absolute gent of a guy.

*Gillian:* My parents were great when I came out. But you could see they were really trying, do you know. It obviously wasn't the easiest thing for them at the start. Now they are the most supportive people in the world. My Mam went around with rainbow flags and all this kind of craic, buying rainbow candles, rainbow blankets and everything. I remember my Dad told my Nanny. She died in 2014, but when he told her, she just said, 'God she must have had an awful weight on her shoulders. Like she must feel a weight lifted now that everybody knows and she can be herself.' And I thought that was brilliant for an older lady to say.

*Lora:* I ended up in Dublin where I started meeting loads of gay people, going out, socialising in the scene and stuff. But I hadn't come out. Absolutely not. I still thought, there's no other gays in the Gardaí. I was in Pearse Street station. I was like, I can't be on the streets because I was terrified that I was socialising in the same area that I was actually working in, and that I would meet someone on the street and they would out me. I was terrified but it didn't stop me going out, I mean there was a bar in the city centre that was really popular but the Gardaí used to raid it regularly. My friends would have to go out beforehand to make sure there was no Gardaí outside when we were leaving. I remember being under the table one night because I thought they were going to raid the pub, the Gardaí were outside. It was just madness. That's why I applied for an indoor job.

*Gillian:* My story doesn't seem half as interesting as yours now.

*Lora:* I wasn't out at home to my parents. My sister knew and she was great. She didn't care at all. I remember one time, after being out we were walking up towards Christchurch late in the night, and we were linking arms, walking along. And some fella goes, 'Lesbians.' And she turned around and says, 'And proud.' I laughed and told her to come on. But she just wanted me to meet someone and be happy. Before the civil partnership we went out shopping with my Mam.

*Gillian:* This was for her dress was it?

*Lora:* Yeah. We were out shopping for her outfit. And I was like, 'It's really important now, because you're a VIP obviously as mother of the bride.' And she goes, 'Well, are you going to be the husband or the wife, or the bride or the groom?' And I was like, 'What?' We're both brides, you know. But she didn't mean anything by it. She just didn't genuinely know.

*Gillian:* And then when you said it to me later on that day, she was nearly mortified that she had said it.

*Lora:* Will you be Gillian's wife or her husband? I was like,

'We will be both wives, you know.' She genuinely was trying to get her head around the terminology. But she couldn't be more supportive. Like she's mad about Gillian. Like when we moved down home I think they are happier to have Gillian down there than me, to be honest.

*Gillian:* Yeah, I'm the favourite daughter now.

*Lora:* We had a lovely day for our civil partnership.

*Gillian:* We had 120 people, or something like that.

*Lora:* We could have had more but we literally…

*Gillian:* …where we had it, we couldn't fit any more people. So we literally had to cut a lot of people out, that was awful.

*Lora:* It was terrible.

*Gillian:* My mother was not happy because the neighbours couldn't go.

*Lora:* Neither of us are religious at all. So we had a very personal ceremony. We had a spiritual ceremony.

*Gillian:* Someone asked me recently, 'Are you going to get married?' And I said, 'After everything we've done on the campaign and everything we've been involved in, of course.'

*Lora:* We certainly wouldn't have been activists in any sort of way.

*Gillian:* No.

*Lora:* But in the build up to the referendum, we felt this

is really important, we had to do something. So we got in touch with Marriage Equality. We thought maybe we could help in the office or whatever. It just kind of went from there.

*Gillian:* For some of the coverage in the campaign, you just had to turn off. It was so upsetting.

*Lora:* I used to watch the Twitter feed and see what people were saying on Twitter to know if it was actually safe enough to watch the TV afterwards.

*Gillian:* It was so upsetting to watch, it really was.

*Lora:* We are out, we are open, we're happy, and we have the support of our friends and family.

*Gillian:* Great support network, yeah.

*Lora:* And I just thought if it's affecting us this much, what is it doing to people who are not out, or who don't have support or whose families have cut them off.

*Gillian:* The result was huge, and you see a lot more couples now after the referendum, up and down the road, holding hands.

*Lora:* You really do, yeah. Guys as well, and it's harder for guys.

*Gillian:* And it is just really nice to see.

*Lora:* We hold hands.

*Gillian:* I'm very conscious of it.

*Lora:* I always slag her. I go, 'You are ashamed of our love.' But we do hold hands.

*Gillian:* We do but you still get people, you know, giving you the look.

*Lora:* But definitely since the referendum, you could see a lot more people being more open. Which is wonderful to see.

Photo: Peter MacMenamin

*Anita Furlong is a counsellor and psychotherapist. A mother of two children she was involved in organising 'Yes Equality' Waterford. Her seventeen-year-old daughter Grace was also active in the referendum campaign.*

# Anita

My story is one that's changed, but it's changed because I've changed. A couple of years ago I would have told a very different story. It would have been far more negative, far less self-assured, far less confident. But now it's a better story.

I was married for nine years. I came out late. I was in my mid-thirties before I came out, and I was married with two young children. They were just coming up to five years and nine years. Within a year of finally saying to myself, 'Yes I'm gay', I had left my marriage. It was really tough. It was very, very tough. I don't like to think about it anymore. The only thing I knew at the time was that I couldn't stay married, that was just not an option.

It was a selfish decision in a sense that I knew I couldn't be there any more. But I also knew it wouldn't have been good for anybody else for me to have been there any more either. It wouldn't have been fair, and it wouldn't have been right. My leaving the marriage was not taken well at all, and still isn't. My ex-husband still doesn't really accept it. We get on fine but if you scratch below the surface there's still an awful lot of resentment and all of that kind of thing there.

Now I look back and say to myself, 'How in the name of God, did I not know?' But I can also honestly say at that time I never even questioned myself, you know, 'Am I gay?' It just never entered my head as a possibility. I suppose part of that would have been my upbringing, strict Catholic family, sheltered middle-class upbringing, not an awful lot of exposure, never met a gay person.

I never really put the question to myself. Now I look and say, well maybe I just always avoided questioning myself. The life I led was quite good in that both my husband and I were involved with horses, that was our passion. And that life covered over a multitude of cracks that might have otherwise appeared in our relationship until there was a year I wasn't busy. That's when I actually had time to stop and think and look at what was going on. I got married at twenty-eight and was married for nine years.

I can look back now, I just had my head buried so deep in denial. I never let it enter my consciousness as a real possibility. At the time I came out, I might have been the only lesbian in Ireland and I was definitely the only married lesbian in Ireland, you know, that was how much I knew of anything.

During the year when I wasn't busy working for the first time in probably fifteen years I had time to start looking at our relationship which was really not going very well at all. What was wrong with it? Why was there no interest physically in my husband or in any other man? And then, I think I allowed myself to start thinking about it. And I allowed myself to start thinking about other women, and then immediately I started recognising, well of course I was attracted to other women before. I didn't realise it at that time. Incredible naiveté but that is what it was.

That year I met a Canadian woman online. I then met her when she was over in Ireland and we had sex. Immediately, I knew, yeah that's it, that's what's missing, that's the difference. I knew there was no going back. I had told my husband I was meeting her and I had told him I wanted to end the marriage. But I was actually still afraid of taking that last step. So we did struggle on for another couple of months, until I finally told him I wanted to leave the marriage. It was really horrible.

I didn't come out to the children for another couple of years. It was a few years, and that was mostly my own struggle with guilt and shame and all of that kind of thing, and fear. I actually lived in fear of them finding out.

The relationship with the Canadian woman was very short-lived. But coming out was the best thing I ever did, without a doubt the very best thing I ever did. My ex-husband mightn't agree with me but I still think it was the best thing for the family as well. I think I would have turned into a terrible person if I had stayed in that relationship. I moved to Waterford. The children lived with me, and went to their dad's every now and again, that kind of thing. I came out to my daughter a few years later. It was something that was slowly building. She kind of realised. I don't even remember a specific moment. I just remember answering a question and saying, that yes, I was attracted to women.

Photo: Peter MacMenamin

*Tommy Roddy is a fifty-one-year-old primary school teacher. He publicly came out as gay after hearing Leo Varadkar's radio interview in January 2015. He canvassed for 'Yes Equality' in Roscommon and Galway.*

# Tommy

There are two threads in my story. There's a story of my coming to terms with my sexuality and the long journey that was. But interweaved with that story, and interweaved with the story of my life, is the story of the mental health difficulties I had in the past and how I overcame depression. The two are very much inter-related. I know some people say that at an early age they would have realised or they would have maybe had doubts about their sexuality. But for me actually I was sixteen, just before my Leaving Cert when I first began to have doubts about my sexuality. I don't know if the word 'gay' was in existence. There were derogatory terms like queer so it wasn't even on the radar. I mean I had these feelings. I remember at the time I had a crush on a boy in my class.

I grew up on a farm and I would have had what could be termed a sheltered existence. So even talking to my parents about anything like that wouldn't have been on the radar at all. Regarding my sexuality I suppose in one sense it was a thread that was there but when I was in college I began to suffer from depression. To cut a long story short it was after my three years in college that I had finished my course and got my qualification but I ended up in a psychiatric hospital. I was very severely depressed. I spent two periods in hospital. I suppose

I dealt with my sexuality in those times by basically denying it to myself even. I would have had some relationships with women at that time and I basically tried to convince myself that I was heterosexual.

The second major crisis in my life happened then in my late twenties. I had moved to Dublin and I got a place on a teacher training course in St Patrick's College. Then my life fell apart totally. The depression came back with a vengeance. It was at that stage then with the process of psychotherapy, you look at all aspects of your life, as well as going back to my childhood and dealing with whatever issues were there. I began to look at myself as an adult and who I was. That was really when I started looking at my sexuality in a serious way for the very first time. They wouldn't be linked from the point of view that my sexuality, or my denial of my sexuality, caused my depression. They would be linked in that my denial of my sexuality among other factors could have been a trigger for the depression. So there would have been a link but it wouldn't have been direct, my depression was not because of my sexuality.

I don't know how many years but I eventually came to accept myself and my sexuality. I remember actually saying it to a friend of mine. He would have been the first friend I would have said it to, and for me to actually say that to a friend was extremely difficult too. I would have talked to him a little bit about my therapy and stuff like that, and I said to him, 'I think I might be gay.' And he was kind of OK about it really, you know. Gradually over time I would have said it to more people.

One of my pastimes is writing letters to the newspapers. I've had letters published in the *Irish Times* and all the other papers. A lot of the letters I used to write at the start were in the area of mental health. So I decided that I would write about Leo Varadkar coming out, and that I would actually state in the letter – just a sentence – 'as a gay man'; and that was effectively my sort of coming out. So I sent that letter into all the papers and the *Irish Times* published it. I wasn't going to tell my mother but then I thought to myself, 'Well, half the country has looked at the letters to the editor page.' So I rang her up. She's in her eighties.

*'There's something I want to tell you.'* 'Yeah.' *'I suppose you heard Leo Varadkar's story?'* 'Yeah.' *'Well there's something I want to say.'* 'Yeah.' *'I'm gay myself.'*

She didn't really say much to that. I forget now her words but it was kind of accepting to an extent. Her problem was the letter to the newspapers. I'd spoken out before about my mental health difficulties, and she had had a difficulty with that.

She asked, 'Why do you have to say all these things in the papers?' I was just up front with her. I said, 'Well, it's part of my journey, it's part of who I am and coming to terms with certain things in my life.' Being able to state this publicly is part of coming to accept myself and all that sort of stuff. That was about it really.

Photo: Tristan Hutchinson

*Breda Larkin is an up-and-coming comedian and actress. She is currently touring her third one-woman show,* Breda's Way. *She comes from Aughrim, Co. Galway and is currently living and working in Cork.*

# Breda

There's a song I wrote when I was just coming out to myself. It's called *You Have a Voice*. I didn't actually know at the time what it was about. It became more poignant to me as I went through coming out. Because it's about, like you have a voice, you have a choice, you know, to lift up your head. When I sing it everyone really likes it. So that's kind of become in a way my gay song, if you know what I mean.

I'm a country girl from Ballinasloe. I grew up rural, a big family. I've a twin sister. I wanted to be a boy when I was younger. I was really sporty. I wanted to do the farm work, silage, everything. I didn't want to knit. It was in the 1980s. I was definitely quite reserved, you know sexually. I didn't feel any sort of pull anyway. I think I was definitely very repressed. I do remember Ellen DeGeneres on the telly. I used to watch Ellen at night. And then Martina Navratilova. We were big tennis fans in our house, and Martina was always winning. And when she came out I remember not really watching her any more. But it was a very no-go area because it was too frightening.

I remember after I had gone on a date with a Russian girl. She was very nice. We went to the cinema. The next day I was at home sitting with my mother. She asked how I got on at the cinema and who I went with. I said, 'Actually, a new friend who I met on the internet. She's a gay woman.' My mother went and got a beer and a cigarette. We never drank or smoked. But we had a glass each and shared a cigarette, sitting on the side of the range. I said, 'I think I might be gay so I'm just going to explore that side of myself without making any declaration.' It was a good moment. My mother is great. She's very open minded.

I went to college in Maynooth, and I signed up for different societies. But I remember walking right past the LGBT and not even looking, not even talking to them. I was just like, 'Eh. No, you know.' I met a lady who sort of pulled me out of myself. I ended up falling in love with her. Then I went travelling after that, and I kept meeting lesbians and, you know, it was great. When I came home, you know, going online and maybe finding a date and going to the cinema. My first big one was Dublin Pride when I met a Canadian girl. We didn't get together or anything, but we became friends. And she introduced me to all her friends up here in Dublin, and I ended up with a Galway girl. I'm still very good friends with her. That was just a huge eye-opener, that first Dublin Pride. I really found my confidence, you know, as a gay woman.

*Brian Sheehan is from Kilrush in Co. Clare. For over two decades he has been an LGBT rights advocate.
He is the Executive Director of GLEN and was a Co-Director of the 'Yes Equality' referendum campaign.*

# Brian

I was born in Kilrush in west Clare, a beautiful part of the world, a lovely place to grow up. Great family, three sisters, one older, two younger. I have distinct memories of being about seven and knowing that something was different. I didn't know what that something was. Obviously I didn't have any name for it for a long time. But I knew. It seems kind of ridiculous but I knew that I was attracted to boys in a way that I wasn't attracted to girls.

In secondary school, I did one year in Kilrush and then four years as a boarder in St Flannan's in Ennis. I had that same sense of being utterly isolated. There was a part of myself that couldn't be spoken about to anyone ever, and whatever 'it' was, it was going to profoundly impact on my life. I didn't know how I was ever going to deal with that. You saw nothing about gay people anywhere. The only people I knew who were gay were David Norris, who was a Joycean scholar, and John Inman from *Are You Being Served?* and I wasn't either of those. I literally knew of no other gay person. I certainly didn't think there was anyone else in Kilrush. I don't even remember seeing much in the press but what was there was always pejorative, that I was a criminal.

I finally got to Dublin when I was eighteen, and it took me another couple of years to find myself. This was in the mid-1980s. I hadn't gone to college yet, I had gone straight into the bank and I didn't know what to do. In Dublin there was Books Upstairs, which was in the George's Street Arcade. And it had whatever *Gay Community News* was called at the time, which were placed on the floor. I remember on a Saturday going in there, walking up and down about for an hour to figure out was there anyone I knew anywhere in the vicinity, and then going in and out and not even picking GCN up. That was all about trying to find an image of myself somewhere, anywhere, just anything that said 'there are others'.

At one point I rang up Gay Switchboard Dublin and I asked them for a psychiatrist or a counsellor. I suppose I wanted it to go away. I didn't really know what I wanted. I went to a counsellor. I sat on a sofa and after three sessions thought it was going nowhere. She wanted to know everything about my childhood and this just paralysed me. Because I couldn't even say it. I remember at one point she asked me to sit in a chair and to face the wall, turning away from her. But I couldn't say I was gay. I just couldn't say it. I probably was about twenty-one at the time, and I just couldn't say it. Because to utter it to somebody would have meant that the gaping hole would then be open right there in front of me.

I ended up withdrawing from friendship networks. I didn't make many close friendships. Because there would have been a fundamental dishonesty at the basis of it. There wasn't a moment in coming out, and that's the point. It was like death by a thousand cuts. And I don't say that lightly. It felt like every time you did it, it was a self-inflicted wound, because you are taking a risk that people may disappear and you will be the one who will be harmed. Not the other person but you. And you will lose something. I remember on one of the Saturday nights when I wasn't going out having a long conversation with a bisexual friend of a friend. She knew I was gay and was waiting for me to say it. I don't know that it felt like a relief when I said it to her but it had taken so bloody long that I was just weary at this point. It's all-consuming in a way. And it was behind everything because it's this huge thing. Through this friend I met her then partner and very slowly started to meet other gay and lesbian people.

I don't remember the dates, partly because remembering those dates means you have to go back, and you have to look at a whole wasted time. I don't really want to focus on that. I mean I got on in my career somehow or other, and I did well in the bank and all that. But there was a whole wasted emotional life. It has an impact on you; those years when you should be learning how to form romantic relationships, how to build networks and how to make friendships. It affects different LGBT people in different ways. But for me it was about pushing people away. And to have to think about that is just too painful. Those years from fourteen to twenty-four, it's just a solid blank for ten or more years.

Eventually I got to know other gay people, I was getting involved in lesbian and gay issues. I was involved with Gay Switchboard Dublin. So I was being more public and being more confident. At some point post-1993 I said it to my sisters. I think they kind of knew anyway, you know. But then with my partner at the time we made a film about HIV and AIDS in Ireland. It was going to be shown as part of the Dublin Gay and Lesbian Film Festival and I could be mentioned in the media. So I knew I had to go down to Clare to tell my parents.

I remember reversing my car into the drive, rather than driving in and reversing out. Because I just thought, 'OK, well at least I could get away quickly if needed.' Rational thought wasn't possible at that point. My parents were unlikely to throw me out or never speak to me again. That's not the kind of people they were. But I didn't know that. I certainly didn't know it emotionally. And, I suppose, I didn't conceive it rationally. I happened to be the last male in the Sheehan line. So there was now going to be no children, the name was going to die, all that kind of stuff.

So I went in, scared shitless. We were in the sitting room. They kind of knew something was up. I actually don't remember what I said but I said something like, 'Look, I have something to tell you, you know, essentially I'm gay.' There was a short pause and I think both of them said that they loved me and that's what mattered. I suppose I wasn't surprised. I don't think it was a surprise really to them. I didn't need to drive home that night. I stayed, and I left the following day. They were very loving.

Let's say that was a Wednesday. My father came to Dublin on the bus on the Friday, and asked to see me. Never done that before, never. I didn't know what to do. I didn't want to have to deal with their working this through because I couldn't support them. I didn't want him to come. But he came. And he apologised for not being what he thought a good father should be. We had never had those kind of conversations. They weren't easy. At the time I just wanted it over but I hugely admired him in a way for doing that. It was a hard thing for him to do. And then to turn around and go back home again. Not something he would ever have done, come to Dublin on his own.

He died in 2001. I had lovely conversations with him as he faded away. He said that it didn't surprise him that I was gay: while he hadn't necessarily thought about it, it was something he would always have known, instinctively, even though he had never focused on it. And he said something lovely. He said he was never disappointed in me. And he said I would make a very good father. And he hoped I would have children sometime. It was a really lovely thing to say.

I think my coming out was a kind of a catharsis for my mother as well. I've never spoken to her about it but this was new and different for her. I think it was probably harder for her than it was for my Dad actually. He was a very accepting man generally. He was the one you always went to when there was trouble, who would mediate with my mother. I think it was harder for her because she also had to deal with some things about herself and feeling responsible for protecting her child. I grew up knowing nothing about gay people. My parents grew up knowing that you had to stay away from 'those people', that they were a bit queer, a bit odd. I never knew what 'a bit odd' meant. Their conditioning was that there was something wrong with people who were gay. And I picked that up. From them and from everyone around me.

One of the unbelievably painful and boring things about being gay is that you've to continually come out. And it's tiresome in the extreme. Each time you do come out you have to pluck up your courage because you don't know what the reaction will be. Most people's reaction to me was positive. But there were one or two people who stepped away or contact eased over time. But I had no hostile reactions. I've never experienced direct physical attacks.

I was out on a date recently and we were walking on Dun Laoghaire Pier. He was a guy from Italy who instinctively took my hand walking down the pier. Now I'm publicly, openly, gay yet I had a moment of going 'let me just check around first'. It's an instinctive thing borne of the fact that you have to unlearn some behaviours. The learned behaviours are about protecting myself from way back when I was seven. That I had to hide my feelings, because they were somehow dangerous to me, and not acceptable in society. I learned that behaviour. Everybody else was learning to be open and to make friends, and to develop relationships of a romantic nature. I was learning how to control and hide. This was my experience and is common to some lesbian and gay, bisexual and transgender people. There was a moment when you realise you are different from everybody else, and you know that you can't be openly different. Former President, Mary McAleese, talked about 'discovering' your sexual orientation, not choosing it. The type of environment in which you discover it is crucial for how you can adjust to it, and how you can successfully build your life, despite, as she called it 'the architecture of homophobia and transphobia' around you.

I always believed that we would win the referendum. For the simple reason that I thought we would find how to appeal to the best in Irish people in a way that would enable a majority to vote yes. For me, it was always about the fourteen-year-old me. For that young person, it was impossible to countenance loosing the referendum. Because for the frightened, scared fourteen-year-old me, and those fourteen-year-old LGBT people all over the country, the idea that the Irish people would say 'No' we couldn't let happen. That was the primary motivating thing for me, we just couldn't let that happen. So whatever it took to win was going to be the only game in town.

Two moments stand out for me in the campaign. One is the Friday of the vote. We are all in the Yes Equality Head Office. We had been monitoring social media all day, and following the journey of the 'Get the Boat to Vote' group coming from London. A video was posted of one of them, Una Murphy, on the deck of the boat as it came into Dublin, singing 'She moved through the fair.' It was extraordinary. We were sobbing. It was so beautiful with the line 'It will not be long love 'til our wedding day.' It was one of those magic moments.

The second moment was the day we handed out the 500,000th badge. Gráinne Healy and I were done up in our finery handing 'Yes Equality' badges out at the top of Grafton Street. A couple of people had come along. Photographs were taken as if they were receiving the 500,000th badge, but there wasn't any magic to it. And then I saw an older man coming up the street and I asked him if he would like a badge. He replied, 'I would be delighted to.' Then I added, 'Would you like to take the 500,000th badge of the campaign?' And he paused and said, 'I would be honoured to do so.'

His name was Vivien Sheehan. He's no relation despite the surname. He was from Castletownbere, I think, but had lived in Windy Arbour in Dundrum all his adult life. He was lovely. He tidied himself up, and fixed his hat and stood there, beaming with delight, being photographed accepting the 500,000th badge. And I just thought, if this charming, gentle, lovely man in his eighties can be so generous to do this, then we've surely won the referendum. And with that, it was clear Ireland had changed. The campaigning had created a space where that wonderful kindness and generosity of Irish people was allowed to shine.

On the day of the count I went to the campaign office first because there was lots to be done and then went to the count centre at the RDS, where there was the media scrum. And then I was taken aback, watching the media, watching the results come in and knowing what this meant, after the campaign for marriage across the last fifteen years. That kind of got me. I think the people of Ireland have probably done more than anything we will ever do as activists in their generosity and with their sense of fairness. Through the size of the majority, and with every single political party saying 'Yes' the Irish people have told us that we, finally, belong in Ireland. Now that doesn't necessarily impact on the mindset of some young man who is fourteen, who hasn't told another human being that he may be gay and who may be struggling, but it does change for the better the environment in which he discovers who he is. It's why some of those voices arguing strongly for a 'No' vote have to carry a responsibility because they are saying to that young person there is something wrong with him still. That's a legacy we have to change.

Photo: John M<sup>c</sup>Colgan

*Adam Hannon is originally from Sligo but now lives in Ballaghadereen in Co. Roscommon with his mother, Joan Dodd. Adam is studying music and french at Maynooth University.*

# Adam & Joan

*Adam:* I'm seventeen I'm from Sligo originally, but I live in Ballaghadereen now. I was fifteen when I came out. It wasn't to let everybody know, it was more that I was comfortable enough in the fact at that stage that I was gay, and the people that I cared most about, they knew. I never sat Mam down, and I never sat down my brother and sister, and I never said, 'I am gay.' For me they always knew, and I knew they knew, and I didn't have to say it. They were so comfortable with me being who I was, like I was very into hair when I was younger and liked doing things with hair. Mam would always let me buy whatever I wanted, not like in a spoilt way, but if I wanted a Bratz doll, I would get a Bratz doll. They were more fashionable than Barbies, that's why I went for them.

I was always gay. For anybody who knew me for a long time, it was no surprise. Like it would have been surprising if I had brought a girl home. My sister said to me, 'Adam, congratulations on coming out, but like I knew. And if you ever brought a girl home that was when I would sit you down and talk to you.'

I didn't have the pain that other people had, like where they have to sit down and their parents haven't got a clue. My friend, he's gay. And he would have had a harder time telling his parents than I would have. I was there to talk to him and stuff, but I also let him know that I didn't have the same experience. So I couldn't sit up on a high horse anywhere and say, 'Oh, this is the easiest thing in the world, you should be able to do this, you know.' Because obviously it isn't. It's about telling your parents something that is a huge factor in your life. And if they don't know about it, it's quite a shock.

I didn't campaign in the referendum because it was during the Leaving Cert. But I did want to. I handed 'Yes' badges out in the school. There was a good response. Now there was one girl, and I knew she was of the 'No' opinion. I only had a limited amount of badges. She asked me for one. And I was like, well that depends. 'Would you vote "Yes"?' And she was like, 'I don't really know Mam is voting "No" and Dad is voting "No" so I will probably go with them.' And I was like, then you don't really need a 'Yes' badge. I will give it to somebody who is going to actually spread the word, rather than somebody who is on the other side. People wanted to be on the bandwagon and when they realised it was fashionable to be accepting of the LGBT community, then that was when she wanted the 'Yes' badge. But I didn't give it to her.

One of my really good friends met this guy in Dublin. He was gay. She introduced me to him. And then we started talking for ages and ages and ages. And then I asked him would he come to my Debs. And he said he would have no problem with it. For me it was the normal thing. I was going to do it because that's what everybody did. They brought their romantic interest to the Debs. It shouldn't have been any different for me. It wasn't as if everyone always thought I was straight, and then suddenly I am bringing a guy to my Debs. Like they knew full well.

I know we got so many looks. But it wasn't in a 'Oh, Jesus Christ' kind of way. People were genuinely interested in the fact that I had brought a boy. You know how usually the girl will wear the dress and then the boy will wear the colour of the dress in his tie or dickey bow. We both wore the same coloured dickey bow, just so people kind of made the association. People were coming up to me and they were like, 'Oh my God, he's so good looking, and he's so cool.' People were saying that I had a lot of courage and bravery to bring a guy. But, at the same time, I wasn't going to do anything else. So it didn't seem like courage and bravery to me at the time. It was very normal. And I would definitely do it again.

*Joan:* I would never have said anything to him to make him feel uncomfortable about any of his little quirks, wanting a doll or putting a tea towel on his head. I would never ever give him a complex or put my worries onto him. The one time I remember when worry came to the fore most was when he started secondary school. In national school he always had great friends, and he was always very popular. He was always very popular with the teachers. Everybody loved Adam. But when I dropped him off at secondary school I remember he was running in, he had a feminine run, and I was thinking to myself, 'How do I tell him if he's running like that, he's in this big bad world now, it will invite comments.'

I would always have talked to him, you know. I was so intent on protecting him and so intent on accepting him, no matter which way he was, that I wouldn't have sat down with him and said, 'You know, there's a big bad world out there.' I didn't want to give him that complex. I would worry when he would go out to a club. 'Oh, what if he comes to the door covered in blood, or somebody has beat him up.' I mean that will always be a worry. But at the same time he's very mature, very streetwise. He's well able to mind himself. Like he's proven that through school, you know, through the way he dealt with people in school.

I absolutely wholeheartedly loved his Debs. I loved it. I wanted to shout from the rooftops. In rural Ireland at seventeen, I thought go Adam. The confidence that he had to do that. I was so proud of him to make that choice, and not to be put off by what would people think. I was so proud of him to do that. Maybe about a year or so earlier when we lived in the country and he was going to school on the bus. For the craic, he says, I am going to go down the back, down to the tough ones, you know, the mouthy ones. And one of the girls says, 'Hey, Adam who are you bringing to the Debs?' And Adam says, 'I might bring Alex from Dublin.' And that just shut her up. She didn't expect him to be so forward and to say it, you know. And that's the way he dealt with any comment like that all the time. And I thought, fair play to you. They wore the same coloured dickey bow. I have a photograph. The same red dickey bow and braces. It was just wonderful. He just didn't make a big thing about it. Do you know? He just didn't. I am incredibly proud of him. I am incredibly proud of his confidence, his belief in himself.

Photo: Peter MacMenamin

*Colin O'Mahony was born in 1984 and grew up in Dungarvan, Co. Waterford. He comes from a family of six. He lives in Waterford City with his partner, Denis.*

# Colin

I came out when I was twenty-one to my family, to my parents, which was probably one of the hardest things that I have ever done. There's always that fear about possible rejection or that it could up-end your whole entire family. I can remember sitting at home, I was actually working at eleven o'clock in the night. It was 10.30pm and I told my Mam, knowing that I had fifteen minutes to tell her and that then I had to go at that point. And thinking there's a genuine possibility that I would never be allowed to go back.

I think deep down I knew that I would be accepted by my family. But you hear horror stories, and that was a good ten years ago now. So things were a lot different back then as well. So I remember telling her and she went, 'Oh God, I thought you were going to tell me you killed someone.' For me, my biggest fear would have been my Dad, you know. It's always different when you are telling your Dad these things. I remember saying, 'What about Dad?' And the response she gave me was the response I was a little bit worried about all along. She said, 'If he doesn't like it, he's going to have to find somewhere else to live.' This all happened in fifteen minutes. And then I went out to work, and I felt like such a weight had lifted off my shoulders. I knew that I had a mother who would do anything for me, you know I always kind of knew that growing up. The next day I came home, she informed me that she had told the rest of my family. She had told them. And my poor Dad, when she told him his response was, 'Sure, what do you want me to do about it? It's not my fault.' And that was it. That was my coming out story.

My family accepted me but, I think, underneath it all they feared for me. Now that I'm older I can see it. My mother feared the possibilities. I think that's something that people who aren't gay have, it's almost like the death of a person, maybe the death of an idea. The idea that my son is going to grow up and get married to a woman and have children and have a house, to 'Oh God, my son is stepping outside the door, what if people attack him, what if he gets sick?' All these things can happen. I would say my mother at the time would have been one of those people that thought that only gay people could get AIDS, do you know? So it's interesting to see how she's changed ten years later. She would have been very supportive of the marriage equality referendum. As my partner says, who I have been with now for five and a half years, he says, your mother wears her gay son like a badge of honour. And she does. And my father does too. He really does.

After we told my father, I think it was in November when I told them ten years ago, and that Christmas the running joke in the house was my Dad joking with my older brother, who is straight, that he was the gay one. Just making all these jokes and having a laugh. It was great because that was how I knew that I was accepted by them. It's not something that my father would talk about. He wouldn't ever question me on it or ever speak about it. But when I go down home with my partner, my partner is treated like a son. Dad looks after him. He'll always give him a nudge and say, 'Are you alright there?' My father went down to Dungarvan to the 'Yes Equality' tour bus. I called my mother the day before to try to get Daddy down. I said it would be really good if we could get some men his age. Like my dad is sixty-four. I was like, it would be great if we could get him down there, you know.

My Dad is a big burly man, and he wouldn't talk about it. And, the funny thing is, I honestly think that if he was in company and people started making jokes about gay people I don't think he would actually say anything. I don't think he'd stand up and go, 'Hang on a second, I have a son that's gay.' I think he'd let it slide. So when he did arrive down I was very happy especially because I actually didn't make it to Dungarvan. So I left him and my mother there all on their own. But he was happy out. I think he was surprised at the amount of other local people that came out in support. And, I think, he kind of felt part of something which was great. There was a picture of him in the local paper holding up the big 'Yes Equality' sign, and that's a really proud moment for me.

*Anne Marie Lillis (L), is a primary school teacher. Her partner, Claire Goss (R) is an IT professional currently working with RaboDirect. Anne Marie is a former chairperson of the INTO's LGBT Teachers' Group. Anne Marie and Claire were involved in the 'Yes Equality' campaign in Leixlip.*

# Claire & Anne Marie

*Claire:* I didn't have one particular coming out moment. I suppose coming out to myself took a long time. A defining moment of my childhood is when I watched *Baywatch* for the first time and realised I was watching the female lifeguards and not the male lifeguards. I would have been like ten or eleven at that stage. So all of a sudden it was just like, 'Oh my God, am I, you know, am I gay?'

When you read all the problem pages in the teen magazines at the time, people would write in with very similar stories, and nearly every single one of those stories came back with the agony aunt, or the agony uncle, always saying, 'It's perfectly normal. These are perfectly normal feelings, you will grow out of them.' Every single comment I read was that way.

The first time, I think, I said it out loud was when I was twenty-three or twenty-four. I said it out loud to a friend, and in the context of, 'I think I might be bisexual.' But I wasn't bisexual, I'm gay. In my early twenties I started getting panic attacks. And these were, I think, directly linked to holding this information inside. I wouldn't have had any major panic attack but I did end up in hospital once with heart palpitations. It was only when I really admitted it to myself that the panic attacks stopped.

I met Anne Marie on the 20 December 2008. I was going out meeting friends for Christmas drinks. I met her that night in the Front Lounge. We were introduced to each other by a mutual friend. And two days later my Mum dropped me off at the train station for our first date. On the way I told Mum that I had met somebody and that we were going on a date. So Mum was literally there from day one. And she often still refers to it by saying, 'Oh, do you remember when I dropped you to the Dart station?'

Within two weeks of first meeting Anne Marie, she met my Mum, my sister and my sister-in-law. I was living abroad in the Netherlands at the time and I knew that my Mum was a little anxious when I told her that I had met someone. So I organised the dinner a few days before I headed back to the Netherlands to alleviate any fears they may have had. But I knew that once they met Anne Marie that everything would be fine. At the time I didn't realise how much of a big thing it was for Anne Marie. It was huge pressure. I don't think it's usual to meet the mother, the sister-in-law and the sister in less than two weeks! And that's exactly what happened. Since we started going out Anne Marie has been part of the family.

Before the referendum when we were walking around town we would have held hands occasionally. But then we would let go for some reason. And we would hold hands again when we felt safe. We were looking around to see who is around or what street are we on, and things like that. But since the referendum you almost feel proud to hold hands. It's a completely different feeling. And from other people you get the nod of approval. You can sense that people love to see it as well.

*Anne Marie:* It's quite emotional listening to Claire there, going back so far. I am originally from west Limerick, a place called Athea, near Abbeyfeale. I'm thirty-eight as well. There's only one month between us. Similar to Claire I would have known since a young age that I was gay. I remember I was in sixth class, and I was eleven. We used to do Irish set dancing in the hall at lunch times on Tuesdays and Thursdays. And I remember one of the boys in my class who I was dancing with saying to me, 'I bet you, you don't know what a lesbian is?' Now I was only eleven but I knew what it was. He was being cool trying to outsmart me and again he said, 'Well what is it then?' I said, 'It's when girls like girls.' I don't know how I knew that but I knew. It must have been the *Late Late* or something! It's funny I do remember we used to stay up watching the Late Late on the Friday night and I do remember the lesbian interview.

Once I admitted it to myself I would have come out to friends in college. It was a big deal. I remember I came out to a friend, who in later years I would be bridesmaid for. I came out to her when we were on the J1 in America. It was funny because we were up late one night after work and I said to her, 'I've something to tell you.'

I didn't know how to say it to her. So I said, 'Do you know the way you like yoghurt? You have different flavours of yoghurt.' I don't know why I came up with this but I started going on about the flavours of yoghurts. I said, 'Well, some people just like strawberry yoghurt, and other people just like hazelnut.' And then I said, 'Some people like both flavours. Well, I only like hazelnut.' Eventually I said it. I don't know if I actually said the words, 'I'm gay' or 'I like girls.' But it all started with flavours of yoghurt. It was only the beginning of the internet back then. I didn't know where to go to or who to go to. I felt very isolated. So Hilary was the first person I told. But it had been in my head for a long time.

That's how I started coming out to friends. After college I started teaching in Leixlip, and I knew from day one, that this was something that could potentially be a problem. I didn't talk about it. I felt like I was the only gay teacher in Ireland. Within the profession it was just not talked about. I didn't know any other gay teachers. There were 180 students in my year in college, and statistically some of them had to be gay but at the time I didn't know any. It seemed to be a very straight world. At one stage I considered leaving teaching because I felt that there was no place for somebody like me in the profession.

I suppose the defining moment was when I saw a notice in the teacher's magazine, *Intouch*. It was back in 2004. And they were setting up a group for LGBT teachers. I didn't know whether to be elated or absolutely terrified when I saw the notice, it was a mixture of both. In my head I was asking myself, 'Do I go or do I not go?' Thankfully as it turned out I went along to the meeting.

It was held in Jurys Inn in Parnell Square, Dublin. I remember it well. It was a dark, wet November evening. The venue wasn't publicised. You had to contact the INTO and only then were you given the details of when and where to go. The meeting was held in private, away from the glare of any media and there was a definite air of secrecy about it. It was certainly something that I would not have attended had it been a public event. Gay teachers is something that is talked about much more now than it was then back in 2004.

Fourteen teachers attended that first meeting as well as four officers of the INTO. That meeting was the first 'coming out' in my profession. I remember walking into the hotel. I was very nervous beforehand. I was wondering, will I meet somebody I know? I remember going in and seeing this group of teachers. And somebody said, 'Oh, come in, we are waiting for a few more.' I didn't dare look around. I just found a seat, I sat down and I kept my head down. I waited for the meeting to begin. The four INTO officials opened the meeting. And at the end of the meeting we were all chatting and it felt like a ray of light at the end of a long tunnel. It was brilliant. I wasn't the only gay teacher. That meeting was hugely significant, that group of people affirmed for me, for the first time, that it was okay to be a lesbian and a teacher.

I didn't publicly come out at school until 2014. That year I addressed the annual INTO congress and spoke about what it was like being a gay teacher. Even though some teachers in my school knew about my sexual orientation, in the staffroom they had never openly asked me about it or spoken to me about Claire. And that was after almost fifteen years working beside some colleagues. I know that this was in no way a negative reflection of them, nor did it show that they were unsupportive. But what it did show was that there was a culture of silence in our schools around minority sexualities that existed for a very long time. Thankfully that culture of silence is changing and LGBT inclusion is something that all schools are now working on.

After my address at INTO Congress that Easter I received nothing but positive messages and huge support from colleagues and other teachers. And that was very affirming. I think people thought they were doing me a favour by not talking about it or maybe they didn't know whether I wanted to talk about it. I take responsibility for my part in all of this as well. But ultimately I was very relieved that people knew. It's like taking a bandage off, the pain is sharp and intense but gone in seconds. It's a fear that you have but there's such relief once you've done it. Because speaking at Congress was a public event I knew that it would be followed up by the media on the radio and in the newspapers. I was a little worried that there may have been some negative feedback but it was all absolutely fine and couldn't have been better. My School Principal rang me literally five minutes after I gave an interview. And she said, 'Anne Marie I heard you on the radio. I just want to say, I'm so proud of you.'

Photo: Syed Talal Ali Shah

*Mark Govern, originally from Tallaght in Dublin, has worked in the finance sector in Australia since August 2014. Previously Mark was involved in the Diversity Champions Programme administered by GLEN. In May 2015 he travelled home to Ireland to vote in the marriage equality referendum prompting the 'Home-to-vote' campaign.*

# Mark

I've been working in Australia in the Commonwealth Bank. The most common question people ask me is why did I leave Ireland. People always assume I left for economic reasons, but I didn't. I left a secure job and I came away for a bit of a personal challenge, that was it. I never went away in my early twenties so I decided coming up to thirty-one that I wanted to go and live away from Ireland for a couple of years when I still have the currency of youth on my side. So in the space of about six weeks I decided I'm definitely going to do this. That was a year before the referendum.

I was involved in the marriage equality campaign, loosely, on the periphery for a long time. And I was conscious going away to Austalia that I was going to miss the campaign. While I was in Australia I kept in close contact through social media. I listened to the RTÉ Player all the time. So I knew exactly what was going on. As it was getting closer to the referendum I was really anxious about it. If I had been at home in Dublin I would have been knocking on doors and canvassing with my friends. I just felt so out of the loop here in Sydney. The best way to describe it was being in a 'Facebook bubble'.

There was a group set up here in Australia called 'Irish Yes Equality Australia'. We got together a few times in the weeks before the referendum. We held a fundraiser, and tried to get publicity. Then it came up in conversation, would we go back to Ireland? I felt I could contribute in some way so I decided probably about six weeks before the vote that I would book a ticket to come home. It was literally that spontaneous. It was something I wanted to be part of, a once in a generation opportunity. I would say a couple of thousand people travelled home from Europe and the UK. So if the result was close they could have made a difference. And I couldn't have imagined if I was in Sydney watching the result or listening to it on the radio, I would have been devastated that I wasn't in Dublin. I have absolutely no regrets about doing it at all. It was a great weekend.

Deep down I was always confident the referendum was going to pass. I would have been absolutely devastated and humiliated if it had been defeated. To put that in context, when you come to somewhere like Australia, a big country, people have this perception of Ireland as a conservative, Catholic country. I mean I'm thirty-two but I wasn't brought up in a conservative, Catholic country. I was brought up in a very progressive, liberal and open country. One of the most international countries you will ever find. So if we had voted down this referendum the incorrect opinion of Ireland that people in Australia and America have, would have been vindicated and validated to some extent. So, you know, the 'Yes' vote really sent the right message out there.

I have four older siblings, four sisters. They are all very supportive about me being gay. There would have been a slight adjustment for my parents, I guess. Like it was unexpected, I suppose. My mother would be a very conservative Catholic although I have to say she has always kept that to herself. I have no negative stories to tell at all. It wasn't something I hid. It wasn't something I wore on my sleeve, but it just wasn't an issue. That was my experience of growing up gay in Ireland.

Both my parents always supported me. My mother would never try and hold me back from anything. She was worried about maybe what her priest would think and some of her friends from the church would think. But I think she was surprised by the reaction to me on Sky News or on Radio One or in the newspaper. I know the priest did say to her that he would say a prayer for me.

A lot of Christians, a lot of Catholics, people of religion, still believe that homosexuality is a sin. If you are a Christian person you probably believe in heaven and by definition does that mean you believe in hell? I don't know. I don't believe in those things. But I fully accept that people do believe in those things. My mother is a strong believer in God. She probably does believe, you know, if I don't confess my sins before I die, that I will probably go to hell. The referendum caused a lot of angst for her.

A few weeks before I came home I put a post on Facebook saying I would be absolutely devastated if the referendum failed. And my Mam saw that on Facebook and I know she got very upset about it. She was completely split. So I think the compromise she came to for herself and her conscience was that she would spoil her vote, which is what she did. My Dad voted 'Yes'. He was a strong supporter of it. And my four sisters were all very supportive. They all voted 'Yes'.

When the campaign was over we all got together. It was actually my birthday. One of my sisters is my twin and our birthday was the week after. So we held that together. We didn't talk about the referendum too much. I guess we just get on with things. But everyone was glad it passed.

Photo: Karl Hayden

*Patrick Dempsey is twenty-three and from the Liberties in Dublin. He currently works with a youth organisation to empower young people. Having campaigned on many social issues the marriage equality referendum had a personal resonance with him.*

# Patrick

I grew up in a place called School Street, the flats in School Street there. It was me, my Mam, two sisters, my Dad kind of moved away when we were fairly young. We would have struggled an awful lot. And I guess we were one of those inner city families that would have been really hit by drugs. Like I mean a lot of my family members would have been on heroin or would have died from drugs. My Mam just tried to help us understand everything that was going on around us. But growing up in the flats was great. It was really, really great craic. All the kids used to be around. Everyone in the Liberties knows everyone anyway. So I really enjoyed my childhood. I enjoyed growing up, especially when I came out. I enjoyed being a young gay person, being able to go to my first gay nightclub with all of my friends on my eighteenth birthday. I had a weird impression of gay clubs. I thought they would all be suited and booted. So when I got there I was very disappointed, and overly dressed. I was kind of, 'Oh, this is just kind of like anywhere else really.'

Growing up I never really felt in myself that I was just like anybody else around me. I don't know why. I felt like something different was happening to me that wasn't happening to other people. From about the age of ten I had begun to start thinking about what it was about, and from about twelve or thirteen I started thinking, 'Am I gay?' My first reaction was, 'Oh, I can't be gay. This isn't happening to me.' I was really upset. No-one else knew until I was fifteen when I finally came out because of my Dad. We were walking through the flats and it came up in conversation. My Dad asked was I gay? I stopped for a second and thought I could either say 'no' and let everything continue, or I could just answer him. So I said 'yes'. He was fine, and he said my Nanny and Grandad were worried about me and wanted me to know that everything would be alright. He asked if I wanted him to tell everything. I thought that would be the easiest thing to do. And after that conversation I never really had anything to worry about. I came out in school in my final year. I had been bullied in school. Some people had called me gay without even knowing I was gay. There was really bad abuse. There would be comments in the classroom and the teachers wouldn't do anything about it. It was very hostile and stressful. But I wasn't lonely.

I knocked on one door canvassing during the referendum, and when it opened, there was a crucifix straight on the wall. And I was like, 'Ok, here we go.' There were a couple of shut doors in the face but you just went on with it. People were also shouting from their balcony, 'Have you got a leaflet, have you got a badge, have you got like a registration form to vote?' It was great that people were so vocally supportive. But you could definitely see the difference in demographic, like in the older population maybe not being as forthright or even not wanting to talk as much about it. I guess the younger people very much got it.

My issue was actually getting people out to vote full stop. My Mam never really voted. She knew how much I had done about the referendum, and on the day she was like, 'I am not going to vote.' And I was like, 'Why?' She was like, 'I don't vote. I don't ever vote.' And she doesn't. My sisters don't vote. My Dad doesn't vote. But I got really really angry, really pissed off. I had to walk away from her. But my two sisters were going to vote for the first time ever so then mam was like, 'I will vote. I was being stupid.' She just wasn't into politics. And actually I think the next day she felt really good about doing it. I went to my mam's, and she was watching the Vincent Browne results, and she was just like 'It's going to be a great day today, isn't it?' And it was because she actually did vote, and other people voted on that great day. But, I mean, it's just hard to get working-class people out to vote.

*Ursula Halligan has had a distinguished career in Irish journalism. She is Political Editor with TV3 News.*

# Ursula

I suppose it started in my teenage years. That was my first real awareness that something was different. I could have been fourteen, fifteen or sixteen when I became aware that something wasn't quite clicking. The whole thrust of the social scene would have been boys and girls. Around this time I would have been aware of feeling, a huge affection is the way I would put it, for somebody in my class, and realising that this was the way some girls might talk about or feel towards a boy. Alarm bells didn't go off then but my feelings were quite intense.

I was trying to make sense of it. All of society seemed to be sending out messages about boy/girl, boy/girl relationships. It was in advertising; in songs, in films. It was everywhere. Yet, my instincts were going the other way. I don't remember anybody discussing the issue. If it was discussed it was always talked about as something awful or horrible. It was either a joke or regarded as some sort of an abomination. But there was no discussion about it like we would have nowadays. It was a no-go area. I kept my fears locked up in my head.

There wasn't a single person I could have talked to. My parents were wonderful, lovely people. But the subject was so 'out there', so off the agenda, it just wasn't discussed. So for me as a youngster I thought I must be weird. In college, and later years, I would hear it being discussed a bit. I listened without contributing. I always thought they are other people, they are not me, I couldn't be those people.

I kept a diary as a teenager. It captured my internal conflict and confusion. I just wrote exactly how I felt which was absolute despair. I expressed all of that upset, frustration, confusion in the diary. Just to get it down, to write it was some relief. I had difficulty writing the word 'gay'. Homosexual or lesbian were words I would have struggled to get my tongue around, even just to say them. It was the worst thing in the world for me to think, 'This is what I am.'

I remember once watching a discussion on the *Late Late Show*. I was in company with a number of people. And one woman said, 'Oh, my God, can you imagine if another woman started flirting with you? How awful.' She was making sort of sick noises. And I remember pretending to be in cool agreement with her and saying: 'Oh, yeah, that would be terrible.' I would have been seventeen or eighteen at that point.

I was hoping to God I wasn't gay because for me that was such a horrible subgroup to be in. I was thinking, it will change. I'm young. You know, I haven't much experience. I just haven't met the right person, the right man. I was praying to be relieved of the confusion and the inner conflict.

When I went to university I completely shut that side of myself down. Buried the whole thing. Closed it. Avoided social situations. Buried myself in work and in books. Over the years I had quite a few boyfriends actually, because the pressure to conform was huge, and they were lovely, really lovely men. I enjoyed my time with them but I never fell in love with any of them. I just conformed. But conforming was difficult. Work and books kept me going. I have a wall of books at home that's testament to those years.

Of course I fell in love with women and never told them. Never told *them*? I never told *me*. I didn't see it as possible at all because I hadn't faced it myself. I had this inner conflict always going on, and while being in love is a wonderful experience, if you are in love and repressed, it's quite a conflicted situation. It's only in the last few years that I have really faced up to it. Whenever I did fall in love I would have thought, 'Oh, here we go again.' Eventually, I did confide in someone. And that was such a big thing for me to do. I could hardly say the words. I went round and round and round. They were saying, 'What are you trying to say?' Saying the words was so hard. And then shortly after that I backtracked. Back into a sort of a denial thing. I buried it again. That was the first time I had ever said it. Looking back, I suppose it was the first little chink.

I told my mother about a year and a half before I wrote my article in the *Irish Times*. My mother was very loving and kind and understanding. I think the reason I told my mother was that it was getting me down a bit. I would say she noticed that I was a bit down. And I felt I needed to explain. I had managed to bury it so much. And that was bothering me. But from an outsider's point of view I don't think anyone would have noticed. I certainly wouldn't have shown it. But deep down it would have been there. I remember feeling a sense of injustice growing, a sense of anger especially at the institutional Catholic church. And then the referendum on Marriage Equality was called and I remember admiring the courage of the people who were promoting a 'Yes' vote.

My denial was so deep though I needed something like a gun to be pointed to my head before I would do anything. The referendum turned out to be that gun and as the campaign got going, I was listening to the arguments for and against, and found myself getting quite exercised about the whole thing. Then, midway in the campaign I read someone analysing the campaign, and saying, if the 'Yes' campaign wanted to make a real impact it needed people to come forward to tell their stories. And while a few people had done so, they needed more. That pricked my conscience. I thought, 'How can I sit back now and leave all the work for others to do?'

I remembered my diaries. I took it step by step. I told myself, I mightn't do anything but let's put an article together anyway, see what it's like and then decide. So, during the Easter break, I went up to the attic and found my diaries. I remember reading them and thinking, 'God, I had forgotten how awful I felt.' Immediately, I started putting down thoughts on paper. They were fragmented, all over the place. I did several drafts. I kept chipping away at it. I have a favourite place where I go in Marlay Park. It's a beautiful walled garden. I have a favourite seat there where I would sit, sometimes for hours, just reading and thinking and soaking up the silence. And it was while there I wrote a rough draft of what I wanted to say. I showed the draft to a friend, and they said, 'Powerful, go for it.'

It was a Sunday evening. I went to tell my Mum what I was going to do. But the following morning I got a phone call from her. My brother, Aidan, had died. This was three weeks before the vote. So I immediately put the article aside. I had actually told Aidan the previous Christmas. We were having a great conversation about something and it meandered into deep areas. I don't quite know how it got into that area. There was a pause in the conversation and I said it to him. His reaction was fantastic. He sprung up from the chair and gave me a big hug. We talked a little bit more. I'm very glad I told him. But it meant then at his funeral the others in the family didn't know. I thought 'the vote is in a few weeks' time now and given I was going to tell them anyway, I'll do it now.' That was the plan. They were all there together. So one by one I went to them. I said, 'I'm thinking of publishing something, I don't know for certain if I'll do it, but if I do I just need you to know about it.' The reaction from all of them was positive.

I was back to work the following Monday. I looked at the piece again. My fears resurfaced. I thought, people will look at me differently. I was equivocating and then I thought it might be too much for my mother, so close after my brother's death. All these things were going through my head, and I was wondering, should I? And then, I got a text from my brother, Peter containing a Martin Luther King quote. It had been a favourite of

Aidan's: 'Our lives begin to end the day we become silent about things that matter.' As soon as I read that, I knew I had to do it.

I rang Miriam Lord from the *Irish Times*, and said, 'Listen, I'm going to send you something and you can tell me if you think I'm crazy.' I was almost hoping she'd come back and say 'No, the *Irish Times* wouldn't publish it.' Instead, she said they would and they took it immediately.

It was a struggle for me to go through this because in my head I saw being gay as second-rate. Second-class. Imperfect. Even on the day the article was published when I was listening to the 'what it says in the newspapers' slot on *Morning Ireland*, I squirmed when I heard the presenter mention the article and say '…and Ursula Halligan in the *Irish Times* tells her story about being gay.'

I will always be glad I published it although I still carry a lot of baggage in my head that needs to be cleared out. I'm working on that. The Irish people were magnificent. Out of generous hearts they enabled a minority to have this crucial right, but it was much more than about marriage. It was about acceptance, it was saying, 'You are OK, actually you are not second class. You are alright.' That for me was the big thing about the marriage equality referendum. What a show of love, empathy, solidarity and humanity. In a way I'm still reeling from it. I can't quite believe it.

People sometimes ask me if I'm religious and I say no, but I do have faith. To have faith and to be religious are two different things. I have a deep faith, a complete trust in a wonderful, loving God who exults in the diversity of his/her creation and loves all of us equally gay or straight. I believe God, as a loving parent, doesn't make distinctions; only humans dare to do that. Religion, by contrast, is a man-made construct that seeks to align itself to God's will but frequently projects its own narrow interests and falls short of the mark. But even here, as in life, nothing is black and white. Despite the anger I have felt towards the institutional church for their treatment of women, gay people and other issues, I also acknowledge the good it does and the many wonderful people inside it who work to make it a better place. Ideally, I would love to find a way of reconciling with the church and I think that will happen when a long over-due reformation of its structures and composition takes place.

I will never forget that the vast majority of people who turned out on Friday 22 May 2015 and voted 'Yes' were Catholic. And I believe they acted in accord with gospel values. I believe God did work through us on that day actually. Afterwards, many people contacted me, including young girls and boys to say my article helped them to start a conversation with their parents or it enabled them to tell their parents or it helped them come out. That for me meant so much.

Photo: Kate Nolan

*Síona Cahill has twice been elected Vice-President for Welfare & Equality with Maynooth University Students' Union. She is a graduate of civil law and sociology and spent a year studying at Boston College. Síona played a major role in the student-led movement for marriage equality.*

# Síona

I'm twenty-three years of age, and I'm from a place called Colehill in Co. Longford. It's a small little parish. There's five of us altogether. I've two younger sisters. I'm the oldest. And my parents, Mick and Carol. I suppose growing up I was the tomboy kid. I was absolutely attached to my go-kart. I used to pedal it up and down to the shop from where I lived. I had an incredibly happy childhood. But I suppose even in primary school I knew that I was different to the other girls. Even at that stage there was a pressure, I suppose, among peers – who do you fancy? who do you like? who's the boy on the scene or whatever? You know, even at like eleven or twelve.

There was one young fella, who played really well on the school GAA team, and he happened to be on the *Longford Leader* one week. I cut his picture out and I put it on my school locker, and I said, 'Now, he's the guy I'm going to say the name of, if I get asked.' Everyone else had a name. So I should have a name too. If the girls were chattering, I do remember, I would have said his name. At least, I was part of the group then, you know. I was the same as everyone else.

I was asked out on two dates in secondary school. The first one was by a guy in my class. We got on so well and we still do, and nothing ever happened. We went to the cinema.

I remember both of our mothers sat outside Longford cinema in their cars chatting across each other's windows with the windows rolled down. I was fifteen years of age. And we went to see *Step Up*. I'll never forget it. He bought me popcorn, we enjoyed the film and came back out and, I think, we hugged in front of our mothers. And that was it. We didn't follow up after that. I was really hurt actually, more hurt than I wanted to be, not because I particularly liked him, but because I wanted some evidence actually, evidence that I could do this, like everybody else, with a guy. I didn't necessarily know at that time was I thinking, it's because he's a guy that this isn't working? I thought it was me. I thought that I was different.

I got asked out another time in secondary school. It was in transition year. We went out probably for two weeks. I had my first kiss with him, with a guy. It was up the back of a bus. He was absolutely lovely and I've no bad words to say about it at all. It was so innocent, you know, but for the fifteen-year-old Síona it was such a big deal. I was heading on a trip to see my uncle for a number of weeks so I called him and I said, 'Look, listen fella, you don't have to wait around for me but I'll see you when I get back.' And he goes, 'Talk to you on the bus.' And that was it. That was the first break up that I ever had. And, I think, I knew after that actually

I didn't have a conversation with my parents until I was in college. I would say I was twenty. They were definitely worried about me. They tiptoed around me for a long time. I'm not sure if necessarily at the time that they might have thought that I was gay but I think that that was potentially there. They were worried that I was unhappy. While I was so full of energy and was always active and always interested, but I wasn't actually doing a lot of it for myself. I was doing a lot of it to distract myself from not really understanding myself that much at all.

There were probably two instances with my mother. Some time in first year in college, and I had yet to bring home a fella or really talk about anyone, we were watching *Grey's Anatomy*. There's a female couple, and I remember sitting on the couch with mum, the fire was on, a winter's night. I exclaimed, I think, at the two women. There was a witty line between the two of them, and I said, 'Oh, that's gas.' I got up to make tea. The kettle is behind where the sofa is in my kitchen. And Mum stayed where she was, and she said, 'Síona, how would you feel about that now?' My heart immediately stopped. I remember standing at the kettle and then immediately flustering about with the milk in the fridge and going into a burst of taking down unnecessary amounts of cups and the sugar, even though nobody takes sugar in their tea in my house.

'*What do you mean, Mammy?*'

'You know, about those two girls there on the TV, what do you think of those now?'

'*Oh, I think they are the best couple on it, like they are class. They've got incredible chemistry, they are unreal together.*'

'And how would you feel about that now, Síona?'

'*What do you mean?*'

'You know, if a girl showed interest in you now, what would you say?'

*'Well, I wouldn't mind if anyone was interested.'*

And then I closed the conversation, and we went back to watching the TV. She didn't push it any further. I think she knew for a long time and was tentatively attempting to bring it up.

I was leaving for a year to go to Boston College. I was so excited. It was after my second year in college. And a couple of days just before I went to Boston Mum was attempting to help me pack or at least get me sorted. I remember she got into bed with me. She was upset because I was going to be leaving. And she asked me, did I think that I was gay? I think she might have said the word sexuality, and the very word sexuality is such a scary term, that I think it took a long time for the two of us to respond to each other actually. And I said to her, that I thought I might be. She was pretty upset. She stayed with me that night. She was a huge comfort. I think she needed the comfort. I think she thought that she was losing a daughter, losing a way of life for me that she wanted, and that she hoped for. And that she was worried about that, if it was the fact that I was gay.

For me it was incredibly confusing because I was in no position to say that I was gay. I just didn't like guys. I had no examples, no evidence really. One of the reasons why I picked Boston College is because Katherine Zappone met her wife there. It might seem like such an odd thing to admit but that was one of the reasons. I suppose I had been watching the 'L word' that summer, looking for role models. The word lesbian terrified me. Absolutely terrified me. I was like, it doesn't feel like it applies to me. I started looking into gay culture on the internet. And I slowly was finding people that enjoyed the same things as I did, and saw the same things as I did, the way I saw them.

I still had more questions than answers. I was really involved with the Obama campaign. I was on the Elizabeth Warren campaign as well. But I realised quite quickly that what I was doing again was filling up my time with everything other than, you know, answering certain questions for myself. It's not easy. How do you do that? Like some people can go out and they kiss a few people on a night out and they are like, Jesus, you know, it's the girls I like to kiss more than the guys. That was unfortunately not something I could do. I wasn't able to do that.

I ended up basically being identified as being quite confused by someone over there who was incredibly confident. She was a little bit older, and realised that I was basically a young gay woman who didn't know herself and her place in the world. She talked to me a lot and helped me come out of myself. I started going to this women's group on a Wednesday evening for an hour. We'd have tea and talk about being lesbian. Sometimes we'd watch a video online about being gay or whatever, and we'd talk about it afterwards. But there was no major dissection.

My first kiss was with a girl called Jenny in Boston. It was at a house party, and she said to me – this was the girl I spoke about before – she said to me, 'Síona have you ever kissed a girl?' I said 'No'. I looked quite horrified at the thought even though my heart was like going ninety, and I really fancied her. I did. I did fancy her. She was so intellectual, so confident. That was always something that I had sought after and never had. I said, 'No' but then she said, 'Well, would you like to?' And I was like, maybe, maybe but in my mind I was like, yes, I do, absolutely, a hundred per cent. But I couldn't really get that out. And then she just literally leaned over and kissed me. I'm not joking you. It wasn't that it was her specifically, or that I fancied her and that she was going to be the one or anything. In fact, I knew that that wasn't going to be the case. But I just suddenly felt at home actually. I felt welcome. And I felt like myself.

Even after my first kiss, I never said I was gay. I never said I was a lesbian. I found it very, very difficult to start saying that. I didn't tell people for quite a while. It was 17 March, St Patrick's Day, and I was the Irish one in the group in Boston. I held a house party. I was going to be leaving pretty soon so I thought it was time that I attempted to bring a lot of my circles together. I had created quite a tangled web for myself, in an attempt to protect the fact that I was gay.

I would lie about where I was going. I wouldn't tell people that I was going to an LGBT meeting. I'd lie by omission more than lie. So I brought my groups together, the study abroad, the Irish crowd and the English and the Australians, and the LGBT who knew me. I just brought them together and just expected them to, by some miracle, understand why they were there in the house, upwards of seventy people. I didn't exactly announce it. I had had a number of alcoholic beverages, and I remember looking down my hallway in my Boston College apartment and saying, 'Lads, this hallway is not very straight.' And one of the girls says, 'Yeah, you're right there.' And I said, 'Because I'm not either.' And that was literally how it came out, by referencing a hallway. I was so nervous, I couldn't get the words out.

I called my Mum after that party on Skype. I was really, really happy, in such good form. We had been through the presidential elections, I had been to the inauguration in January. Things were incredible for me, in loads of ways. I knew how lucky I was to be there. I told Mum I was going to this group on a Wednesday. I had just come home from a meeting when I called her.

'What's this group about Síona?'

*'Oh, you know, it's just a group of girls, chatting, hanging out and stuff.'*

'Síona, is this group about your sexuality?'

It was Mum trying to be educated. She told me after the conversation that she had tried to educate herself about what I might be going through. She went up to Dublin and bought books in book shops about being LGBT. So she asked me, was it about my sexuality?

*'Actually it is, yes. Look, I'll tell you now Mammy, I won't be bringing home any lads from the States.'*

'Síona, that's absolutely fine. You know myself and your father love you no matter what.'

It was just such an easy conversation in the end. So few words were said but it was a really big deal.

I went home to Longford to canvass during the referendum. It happened fairly suddenly. I was worried about going down to Longford. When you come out in college or with friends it is relatively containable. It might be a confusing time but it's a supported time. But in a rural area like Longford its different. I knew people from my community would see me. There would inevitably be something written in the local newspaper. But I decided that I owed it to myself to be part of the campaign. I had worked so hard in Maynooth and in Dublin that it would have been wrong not to go to my home county. So I got on the bus and on the way down I rang my dad. I told him I would be in the market square at twelve noon with the 'Yes Equality' bus. I said, 'If you're around, I'd love to see you.' But I didn't put any pressure on him. I'll never forget when we arrived. I got off the bus and he was standing there waiting for me. He had brought some people with him. He gave me a hug and asked for one of the 'Vote Yes' badges. When I had come home from America he would have preferred that I hadn't got involved in LGBT campaigns. Not that there was a problem with me being gay. He was protecting me. He didn't want me to get hurt. And then nine months later he was standing outside the 'Yes Equality' bus in Longford. That was such a big deal.

Photo: Karl Hayden

*Sabina Brennan is a psychologist in Trinity College, Dublin where she leads a dementia research programme. Her son Gavin is a contemporary-classical saxophonist, concert curator and founder of Modern Irish Music.*

# Sabina & Gavin

*Gavin:* I'm a classical contemporary saxophonist from Dublin. I do a lot of performing, curation of concerts, you know, trying to make my own little career path in music. I am a gay man, but there's several things I would call myself before I would reach that point, to be honest. I was never involved in the LGBT scene before the referendum. I didn't want to be defined by just one aspect of my life. But then when the referendum came about I felt I couldn't expect people to vote 'Yes' for me if I didn't let them know how much it meant to me. So that's really how I kind of stepped forward a bit. In hindsight I kind of always knew I was a bit different, but I always enjoyed being different. Sometimes if everyone's favourite colour was red, I always wanted to be a different colour. If everyone supported the same football team, it kind of gave me an incentive to support a different one. So yeah, I've always been different.

*Sabina:* I'm Gavin's Mum, and Darren's Mum as well. I live in Clontarf. When Gavin went to secondary school 'gay' had just become a negative word that was used like, 'Oh, those trainers are gay.' Kids had started using it to mean naff, not nice, those kind of things. So Gavin was upset because of that. He was saying to me, why are they saying those things about me? So I had this dilemma. Well do I say, 'Sweetheart it's because…', and it was a terrible dilemma, because if he wasn't gay and I said, 'Well maybe it's because you are gay', well then I could be stirring up all sorts of things. So I just always left it very open and just talked about how the boys who did these things had a need to bully or they were doing these things to make themselves feel good about themselves.

*Gavin:* When I got to secondary school, like to be honest, I had people telling me I was gay before I even told myself. More from a bullying point of view. It's kind of funny that a lot of bullies in school, they had a really good gaydar to be honest. It was straight up verbally saying I was gay or much stronger words. Or you would go into the bathrooms and see stuff written on the walls about you or on desks. I don't remember too much of it myself. There were a couple of times I came home very upset, in floods of tears. But you do develop a thick skin. I did have very good friends. So I didn't let it destroy me.

*Sabina:* I went down to the school and I said, 'Are you aware that they are writing this about Gavin in the school? They are writing on the walls, in the toilets. Are you aware of this?' And they said, 'Oh, what are they calling him?' And I said, 'They are saying Gavin is gay.' And they said, 'Oh, Mrs Brennan don't worry about that. They don't mean Gavin is gay as in homosexual. It's just a word they use when they say Gavin is not cool.' And I went, 'Are you for real?' It still blows my mind to think that a head principal and a head of year thought that they were reassuring me saying that the boys didn't think my son was homosexual, and that somehow that was OK.

*Gavin:* My parents are very intuitive as a lot of parents are. They knew long before we ever kind of openly talked about it. But they are fantastic facilitators and I couldn't have asked for anyone else, you know. The door was always open for me to talk about it whenever I wanted to. It was a brilliant family dynamic from that point of view.

*Sabina:* Over the years there were times when Gavin was stressed and wasn't well. I would open the door to his bedroom and I kept saying to him, 'Gavin are you sure there's something not worrying you? Are you sure there's something you don't want to tell me? I'm here, come tell me.' And he would say, 'No, I'm fine, I'm fine.' So it took Gavin a long time.

*Gavin:* It took me a while to be ready myself. I think the way my parents handled it was perfect because you do always have to leave it to the person themselves, for when they are ready. I can only imagine if I was fourteen and everyone sat me down and said, 'Look, we know you are gay.' That would have been a bit tough for me, and I'm sure it would be for a lot of people.

*Sabina:* When he started going out with Jamie, he said, 'I'm going on a date, and it's not with a girl.' And I said, 'Great. I'm so glad that you eventually decided to say it, you know.'

*Gavin:* In the referendum campaign I found it really difficult to go to a stranger's door and ask them to say, 'Yes', so I can be the same as them. Other people would be better at that. So I decided to find my own way to appeal to people and to get my point of view across. I'm a saxophonist but I sing as well, so I decided to record a Youtube video as my appeal to people. There's this song by the band, Magic, called Rude. It's about a guy asking his girlfriend's dad for her hand in marriage. So I decided to change this song, to put an LGBT twist on it, kind of like me asking a nation for the permission to marry. So that was great for me. I figured it was going to get a few hundred views. But it ended up getting a thousand within a week. When I was at the 'Yes Equality' launch, I actually had people coming up to me saying, 'You're the guy from that video.' That was kind of cool.

*Sabina:* I was very scared that the referendum was going to be defeated. That's why I devoted every single bloody waking hour while having a full-time job. I mean I was up during the night. I wrote letters to the newspapers. I set up a Facebook page. I put myself out there. I started using Twitter as I realised that it was really a powerful tool for something like this. But then you really see the vitriol, the nasty stuff online. People were saying nasty stuff. And so I kind of realised, I have to get off Twitter, get out there, knock on doors to really make this happen. One of my first times, I knocked on this door, said what I was there for, and a man about 42 told me to get away from his door. People saying some really nasty stuff. Nasty stuff to hear when you are a mum. It's hard to hold anger in on some of those ones.

*Gavin:* To be honest, I view Ireland differently because of the 'Yes' vote. The number voting 'Yes' was great. But it was more the campaign that changed my perception and made me think better of Ireland than the number voting 'Yes'. Just the positivity from people, everything from letters in the newspapers, to different public events to two girls kissing in front of a homophobe who was quoting God. It just felt like a good place to be. Everyone around the world seemed to have the impression that our Ireland is full of drunkards, full of chancers. So it was nice to get rid of those incorrect pre-conceptions and just say, 'No, this is actually a cool place to be. We're trendsetting, leading the way on a human rights issue in the world.' Being the first country to get to vote on marriage equality was pretty cool.

Photo: Peter MacMenamin

*Luke Barber is a fashion designer from Buncrana, Co. Donegal. His friend Alan died in 2005.*

# Luke

Alan and I knew each other since we were kids. Where my family home is, Alan's family home was just across the road and down in an estate. I was a few years older. As we got older we sort of grew closer. Obviously at the time I knew I was gay and Alan knew he was gay. So we had that in common. And as far as we were aware at the time, there was just the two of us in Buncrana. I am not saying we were the only gay men but as far we knew we were. It was very hush, hush. Being gay even in the early 1980s was something that was still very much frowned upon in our town. We just lived our lives as best we could in secret, if you like. Personally I didn't come out to my parents until I was about twenty-five and I had moved away to London. Alan and I both did.

Alan and I went about our business, we hung out together, we went to pubs. We had a bit of a relationship, you know, but it was more close friends than anything else. Everyone knew us. We were like each other's shadows, and we would hang out together. We were always seen together.

The abuse was constant. At school, at work, even in the pub. There wasn't a week that you didn't get verbally abused. I couldn't pass the local shops without kids calling me a poofter or a queer, or something might be thrown, a stone or a can. I hated being asked to go to the shops. It used to take me ages because I would be weaving from one side to the other to avoid contact. As a result an errand that should have taken me ten minutes might take twenty minutes. I never told my mother because I wanted to protect her from knowing about the abuse.

For about a good year Alan and myself talked about moving away. I remember when we made our decision to leave. There are beautiful beaches here in Buncrana, and we always walked the beach, always talked and walked, summer and winter, you name it. We stood on the beach one day. I think we both had had enough. The previous weekend we both had been attacked physically and there had been verbal abuse by these guys from the town.

We were at our wits end really. We needed to do something about it. I will never forget, we stood and looked out onto the sea. And we embraced because we were both quite upset, and we were trying to comfort each other about what had happened. We felt we couldn't tell anybody, I remember we just made a decision. We set a date that we were going to leave Buncrana. And we did. I think we left on 9 January 1991 for London.

I lived in London for about fourteen years. Little did I imagine that I would be staying that long. Alan was younger than me and, I think, he found it a bit tougher at the beginning and was quite unsettled. So he moved home about seven or eight weeks afterwards. He missed his family. Obviously he had a very loving family, a very close tight-knit family. And they missed him and he missed them. But I stayed, and I stuck it out. Alan came over a few times. I can't remember now but he eventually ended up living in London for about seven or eight years, or maybe longer.

We kept in contact. Usually I would text him on a Monday, and I would ring him every Monday night or a Tuesday night. I always knew if he was on a down day because there would be no contact. You learn to respect that, and you also learn to keep your distance but check in. And on that Monday he didn't respond. I tried a couple of times that day, no response. And then on the Tuesday evening my sister rang me to tell me Alan was dead. And although I knew at times Alan was extremely vulnerable, he was my best mate so it was like somebody had just ripped the heart out of me. He was my leaning post. Like we were each other's armour if you want, even though we were older and had moved on and things were starting to relax a bit. It was just gut wrenching. Really it ripped the heart out of me.

Photo: John McColgan

*Erney Breytenbach (L) and his husband, Vivian Cummins (R), have been foster parents to sixteen-year-old Brandon (centre) for over ten years. They have lived outside Athy in Co. Kildare since 2001. Erney, a former diplomat, is now a psychotherapist/counsellor and Vivian is an architect. They married in December 2009. Brandon is a secondary school student with a keen interest in sports especially athletics, rugby and tennis.*

# Vivian, Erney & Brandon

*Vivian:* I had just moved back to Ireland having worked in the UK for about six years, and one Saturday evening I was out in Dublin. Erney was visiting from Norway, where he was based as a South African diplomat. And we met. Initially I wasn't interested in a long-distance relationship. I had just come back to Dublin and I kind of thought, 'I want to settle and meet a nice Irish man. This is just too messy and complicated.' It was also pretty expensive to get to Norway. So nothing happened for about six months. And then it was Erney's fortieth birthday. We have very different versions of what happened. He said I invited myself. My view is that I was invited. But anyway, I ended up at the party, and it seemed to rekindle things.

I had no qualms about settling down as a couple in Dublin. But part of the terms of Erney moving to Ireland was that we would live in a rural area. He had enough of city living and wanted open, quiet space with vistas of water, trees and animals. I thought it was going to be difficult – a same-sex couple in a small rural area. But I was completely wrong. The neighbours just couldn't have been better. They were very supportive. Some local gay guys did comment on the fact that we didn't pretend to be anything other than what we were. And people respect that. You didn't try to pull the wool over their eyes and pretend you are not gay. This was in 2001.

Fostering Brandon was a kind of a spur of the moment. They say when fostering you are giving, giving, giving whereas I think we just got, got, got out of the whole process. It's been amazing, an absolutely amazing experience. I would say that when we first fostered ten years ago there probably were people who said, what's this about? I would say maybe if you did a survey ten years ago, and asked do you think two men should foster a child, a lot of people might just have said: 'no, I am not so sure about that.' But based on what they have seen I think they'd now say, 'My God they are doing a better job than most parents or look at that kid, he's turned out pretty well.' People are a bit more familiar and comfortable with the idea, and that's the sort of thing that got the referendum across the line.

I never thought the referendum was going to be won until about a week beforehand. We laugh about that ourselves because I am a very glass half empty person, and Erney is a very glass half full. I used up a lot of unnecessary energy as a result. I was conscious that the divorce referendum outcome (in 1996) was so tight, literally every vote counted. I was constantly haunted by the idea that the referendum would be lost.

It would have been devastating. It was like a potential nightmare scenario to the extent that I wished we weren't even having the referendum. I almost thought I couldn't cope with the country saying 'No'. For us personally, for our family, it was just, you are not really a family, you are not, you are just not. During the campaign I didn't sleep very well. I was waking up at 5.30am or 6.00am, which isn't typical. I was so anxious about the result. It was so important.

We were married in South Africa but I would never say to people that I was married. So if I met somebody in Ireland for the first time and they asked me, are you married? I would never say, yes. Because they would then ask, what does your wife work at?

It's a bit like coming out in a way. It's hard to explain.

Not long after the referendum was passed there was a work social event and Erney came along with me. He wouldn't have had any involvement with a lot of these people there. I introduced him to this guy, Bob. Now I just said, Erney, and then I went off talking to some other people. Erney and Bob were joined by another guy. And Bob said, 'Oh Joe this is Erney, Vivian's husband.' Now it doesn't sound like a whole lot but for me that was really, really meaningful. It was the first time a third party had actually referred to Erney like that in Ireland. It was significant.

*Erney:* We talked about children. We both like children. I said to Vivian that I would like to have my own child but it's too complicated. Surrogacy is too messy as far as I am concerned. So really, children were just sort of talked about in general. Then one day he came home with the local newspaper, and he showed me an advertisement from the HSE. They were organising an information meeting for potential foster carers. Vivian said, 'Why don't you phone them and see if we can come to this meeting?' So I phoned the HSE and said, 'I am in a same-sex relationship with my partner and we have seen the advertisement about fostering, can we come to this information meeting?'

The lady on the other end of the line said, 'Oh I am not sure. I will find out, and I'll come back to you.' She rang back within fifteen minutes and said, 'As far as I could establish, as a same-sex couple, you are welcome to come.' Almost like, but I would like to come and meet you too, kind of you know, you get that – like this is quite something.

So we went to the meeting. There were a fair number of middle-aged straight couples. The HSE talked in general about fostering. And at the end of the meeting they said should couples be interested in fostering, then put your personal details down and they would contact us. That is how the whole entire process started. As far as we know, we were the first male same-sex couple who started fostering through the HSE in Ireland.

You do everything that a parent should do, everything that the child needs. I have stood in rain, hail, wind and snow on the sideline of the rugby field, watching him play on a Saturday morning and swearing 'Why the hell do I do this, when I could be warm in bed?' But I do it for him, because I love him. You just do these things. And of course you shout and rant at him from the sideline. Run, run, run, get the ball, tackle him! Through winning, losing, laughter, tears, sad and joy you are so proud of him, because he is my boy and I love him unconditionally.

***Brandon:*** When I was younger I was put into foster care. I ended up with Vivian and Erney. My birth mother approved. I liked them. I have been fostered for ten years now. It is different, kind of like having two Dads but then, at the same time, having two Mams. It was hard to get used to at first. But now, there's nothing different.

When I am with my mates I just say, 'They're my foster parents.' I would never say 'Dads' because I have never really had a father figure. I would say they are more foster parents than anything else.

I definitely know that some people talked behind my back. But it doesn't bother me. They have never been exposed to this. They have never come across a guy who's been fostered by a same-sex couple. It doesn't affect me. Sometimes people ask me, 'What's it like or is it different or what's it like not having a mother.' I just answer the questions.

The first time I told people I got some hassle. Someone said, 'Oh that means you are going to end up gay as well.' But I stood my ground. I replied, 'That's uncalled for. That's stupid. What's the point in saying that?' And then that person kind of understood.

Some people were kind of intrigued. They'd say things like, 'Oh wow. That's different. It's cool.' And when my mates came to the house to actually meet Vivian and Erney for the first time they are like: 'Those guys are genuinely nice.'

Vivian and Erney come to my rugby matches and to athletics to support me. They bring me to all my training sessions. They are there for me. I don't think people pay attention to it really. I don't think they go, 'Oh, they are gay or that's different or whatever.' They probably just glance and say, 'Oh, two men'. But I don't think people are looking or commenting or saying anything.

I have great respect for what they did in fostering me. They kind of saved my life in a way. Like they provided for me when I needed it and they gave me everything they could. I was in a dangerous position when I was younger. It was a bad place. It was pretty rough. And then I got taken out of there. I consider that my life was saved.

It's ten years now. I have been in care with a gay couple more than I was with a normal mother. I have been with them longer than I was with my actual mother. So this is like a normal thing to me. I just wake up, and they are there. So it's no different to me now.

When I had my sixteenth birthday [in October 2015] they sent out the email invitation, and they obviously told everyone that they are two same-sex men. But nobody cared. Nobody questioned. Nobody said, 'Oh you can't go because they are same-sex.' So everyone knows about it and nobody questions it.

When Vivian and Erney got married in South Africa, the ceremony was in our house there. There was a little altar, a tiny little wooden thing. I was at loads of weddings when I was younger. But they were always a man and a woman, and stuff like, you may kiss the bride.

We had this little seashell. So I suggested, 'Why don't we put the rings in the seashell.' It will be a cute thing to do. At the ceremony I brought up the rings in the shell. Everyone was going, 'Ahh'. And then Vivian and Erney took the rings. I loved it.

We played songs. And then someone would speak and we would play another song; and then another person would speak, and we'd play another song. Then Vivian and Erney said their vows, or whatever you would call it. It was all very emotional. Everyone was kind of teary. It was happy, and it was sad. There were all these emotions.

Because they are already married I wasn't that interested in the referendum. I knew it was a massive thing for the nation and for Ireland to be the first country in the world to vote 'Yes'. But I hated every minute of Vivian's and Erney's involvement in the campaign. They were so wrapped up in it. For two or three months everything was about the referendum – it was just constant referendum. Like if I needed to go in my mate's house, or I wanted to go play rugby, it was, 'we have to do this. We have to finish this for the referendum.'

Sometimes one of them is the woman in the family and the other one is the man. And then sometimes it switches. Like Erney is more of the cook in the house. And that's usually associated with women. It's sexist to say that, I know. Vivian likes to be in charge more. He is the one who goes to Erney with all the problems and with suggestions about everything. So in that way Vivian is kind of the woman. So it's different. It changes but they are both kind of motherly and fatherly figures. It's kind of half and half. It would be tough at this stage to imagine life without them. I find love a strong word. It's just strong. I do love them and I don't. It's different. I would say I do, yeah, because they are like family now. Not like blood, but by heart, and they are family now.

# *Acknowledgements*

The idea for this book came from my involvement with the 'Yes Equality' campaign during the marriage equality referendum in 2015. Encouragement from Noel Whelan, Brian Sheehan and Gráinne Healy set me off on this journey. Along the way I got the assistance of many people especially Eimear O'Reilly from 'Yes Equality', John Paul Calnan in Cork, Michael Hennessey in Waterford, Dave Cuddihy in Limerick, Beibhinn O Connor in Galway and in Ballinasloe, Regina Divilly and Kathy Walsh.

Bride Rosney asked me to get involved with the launch of the 'Yes Equality' Campaign. Bride has played no small part in getting the overall 'A Day in May' project up and running.

Proceeds from this book – and the accompanying activities including a play and photographic exhibition – will go to the Day in May Trust. All proceeds will go towards *Console*. I want to thank those who agreed to join the 'A Day in May' Trust – Bride Rosney, Bill Hughes, Brian Sheehan, Ed Mulhall, Kevin Rafter and John McColgan. Pauline Fitzgerald from Fitzgerald & Co. Solicitors has been the legal advisor for the overall project. The Trust would like to acknowledge financial support from The Atlantic Philanthropies in the publication of this book.

A significant number of people have been involved in bringing the book idea to publication. I would like to acknowledge the work of the six photographers whose images feature in these pages. A big thank you to all of them – John Minihan, Kate Nolan, Tristan Hutchinston, John McColgan, Karl Hayden and Peter MacMenamin. Thanks are also due to Colm Tóibín for writing the Foreword. Even with his busy schedule Colm was happy to be involved.

My association with Kevin Rafter goes back a long way. Kevin played a central part in the writing of my biography in 2006 and he has again come to the rescue with the editing and writing of this book.

A special thank you to Dominic Turner from Exhibit A Studio's and Adam May from Language. I cannot thank Adam enough for everything he has put into the design of the book. Thanks also to Clío Meldon from Language who has been involved in the design process. Thanks also to Conor Graham, Publisher, Peter O'Connell, agent and Paula Fagan who read the manuscript.

The overall project would never had happened without the help and encouragement of Martin O'Brien. Thanks also to Karl Hayden for the cups of coffee and the encouragement not to give up on the idea of this book and Su Watson who did a magnificent job with all the transcripts for the overall project.

Thank also to John McColgan and Pat Moylan for their work on the play based on the interviews and stories I recorded during 2015, many of which are included in edited form in this book. My friend Ed Mulhall put me in contact with Colin Murphy who has written the play. Colin's initial reaction to the stories which he read encouraged me to develop the play.

This project would not have happened without the help of the very many people who gave me their trust and told me their stories. Not all the stories are included in the book. Some people for reasons I well understand decided not to be involved in the book but they have allowed their stories to be used anonymously as material for the play. To all of those people who I met and spoke with – this is your book. I see it as a co-operative effort between a group of like-minded people who want to celebrate the historic vote in the marriage equality referendum in May 2015.

Finally, to Claire – or 'Mould' as I call her – thanks for putting up with me while I've been working on this project.

Charlie Bird
March 2016

# Photographers

### John M<sup>c</sup>Colgan

### John Minihan

### Kate Nolan

### Syed Talal Ali Shah